An Introduction to English Poetry

An Introduction to English Poetry

JAMES FENTON

VIKING
an imprint of
PENGUIN BOOKS

VIKING

Published by the Penguin Group
Penguin Books Ltd, 80 Strand, London WC2R ORL, England
Penguin Putnam Inc., 375 Hudson Street, New York, New York 10014, USA
Penguin Books Australia Ltd, 250 Camberwell Road,
Camberwell, Victoria 3124, Australia
Penguin Books Canada Ltd, 10 Alcorn Avenue, Toronto, Ontario, Canada M4V 3B2
Penguin Books India (P) Ltd, 11 Community Centre,
Panchsheel Park, New Delhi – 110 017, India
Penguin Books (NZ) Ltd, Cnr Rosedale and Airborne Roads,
Albany, Auckland, New Zealand
Penguin Books (South Africa) (Pty) Ltd, 24 Sturdee Avenue,
Rosebank 2196, South Africa

Penguin Books Ltd, Registered Offices: 80 Strand, London WC2R ORL, England

www.penguin.com

First published 2002

4

Copyright © Salamander Press Limited, 2002

The acknowledgements on p. 138 constitute an extension of this copyright page.

The moral right of the author has been asserted

Set in 12/14.75pt Monotype Bembo
Typeset by Rowland Phototypesetting Ltd,
Bury St Edmunds, Suffolk
Printed in Great Britain by Clays Ltd, St Ives plc

A CIP catalogue record for this book is available from the British Library

ISBN 0-670-91100-3

Contents

1. The History and Scope of English Poetry

English poetry begins whenever we decide to say the modern English language begins, and it extends as far as we decide to say that the English language extends. We cannot expect everyone to agree with us when we make a decision in either case. Some people, for instance, think that English poetry begins with the Anglo-Saxons. I don't, because I can't accept that there is any continuity between the traditions of Anglo-Saxon poetry and those established in English poetry by the time of, say, Shakespeare. And anyway Anglo-Saxon is a different language, which has to be learnt like any foreign language. Anglo-Saxon poetry may be extremely exciting and interesting, but it excites and interests me (when it does) in much the same way as the Norse sagas excite. It is somebody else's poetry.

What then of poems written in a language that is semi-comprehensible as English, the language for instance of *Sir Gawain and the Green Knight* (which was written some time around 1375)? Or what about the poems of Geoffrey Chaucer (*c.*1343–1400)? These surely count as English poetry, do they not? My answer is that they do indeed count as English poetry, if you wish. But they fall slightly outside the limits I would propose. The language of the *Gawain* poem comes and goes, baffling and comprehensible in turns:

> Queme quyssewes then that coyntlych closed,
> His thik thrawen thyghes with thwonges to tachched;
> And sithen the brawden bryné of bryght stel rynges

> Umbeweved that wyy, upon wlonk stuffe,
> And wel bornyst brace upon his both armes,
> With gode cowters and gay, and gloves of plate . . .

(lines 578–83)

A part of the meaning of this can be guessed. But who, without specialist help, could arrive at the conclusion that someone is here putting on his armour, and who could guess the meaning of 'queme quyssewes' (pleasing thigh-pieces) or 'wlonk' (noble, glorious, fine)? Who could guess their pronunciation?

With Chaucer we are much nearer home, both linguistically and in terms of poetic practice.

> Owt of thise blake wawes for to saylle –
> O wynd, O wynd, the weder gynneth clere –
> For in this see the boot hath swych travaylle
> Of my conning that unneth I it steere.
> This see clepe I the tempestous matere
> Of disespeir that Troilus was inne:
> But now of hope the kalendes bygynne.

(*Troilus and Criseyde*, Book 2, lines 1–7)

Most of this can be guessed, although there is a word-order problem in lines 3–4: 'For in the sea the boat of my ability ("Of my conning") has such difficulty that I can scarcely steer it.' Even when this has been pointed out to us, we find it hard to know whether the strange word order came naturally to Chaucer or was a sign of his incompetence. We need to acquire certain skills in order to read and appreciate such verse.

Some time around the reign of Henry VIII (1509–47), English poetry – some of it – becomes graspable in a newly direct way. We no longer need to look everything up, or worry overmuch about pronunciation (and therefore scansion). It is not that we can dispense with notes, or with the help of our teachers the scholars, altogether. It is just that with sixteenth-century poetry we recognize much more of the language we still speak, and this is encouraging.

The simplest poems in most languages are its songs, and it is in the Elizabethan lyric that we will find many of the earliest English poems we can most easily grasp:

> Followe thy faire sunne, unhappy shaddowe:
> Though thou be blacke as night,
> And she made all of light,
> Yet follow thy faire sunne, unhappie shaddowe.
>
> Follow her whose light thy light depriveth:
> Though here thou liv'st disgrac't,
> And she in heaven is plac't,
> Yet follow her whose light the world reviveth.
>
> Follow those pure beames whose beautie burneth,
> That so have scorched thee,
> As thou still black must bee,
> Til her kind beames thy black to brightnes turneth.

> (*A Booke of Ayres*, 1601, No. IV)

These verses are from a song by Thomas Campion (1567–1620). The music survives, so we can tell exactly what rhythm was intended, that 'scorched' was pronounced with two syllables, 'beames' with one, and so forth. But we could easily have guessed such things even without music.

This does not mean, of course, that the poem holds no mysteries for us, and no opportunities for misunderstanding.

The characteristic Elizabethan contrast between the whiteness of the loved one and the blackness of the lover does not imply a lover of African origin. It implies only an unfortunate lover, a melancholy man whose suit has so far been rejected, but whom the poet encourages to persist. The simple lyrical idea of following the sun was used in the last century by the Beatles in the song 'I'll follow the sun'. The contrast of black and white was used by W. H. Auden (1907–73) in one of his imitations of the Elizabethan poetry for which he had a great fondness:

> O lurcher-loving collier, black as night,
> Follow your love across the smokeless hill;
> Your lamp is out, the cages all are still;
> Course for her heart and do not miss,
> For Sunday soon is past and, Kate, fly not so fast,
> For Monday comes when none may kiss:
> Be marble to his soot, and to his black be white.
>
> ('Twelve Songs, II')

This was written in 1935, for a documentary film about the coal industry. Like the Campion, it is a song. Both Benjamin Britten and Lennox Berkeley have set it to music, the former giving it to a female chorus. The charm of 'Madrigal', as the poem was once called, comes from the contrast between its centuries-old idiom and its grimy contemporary (1930s) setting. 'Black' is used in Campion's manner, but without his meaning.

Let us say that we have about five centuries of English poetry behind us. This poetry did not emerge out of nowhere, but the fact is that beyond those five centuries ago it becomes increasingly difficult to comprehend, whereas within those centuries people use strikingly similar vocabulary, grammar, poetic forms and metres. It is true that to understand Shakespeare (1564–1616) in detail, we need the help of notes, and it has been true at certain times in the past that readers have found large parts of Shakespeare incomprehensible or barbaric. The current assumption that all the plays are in principle both performable and worth performing is comparatively new.

But the really striking thing about, say, the recent film of *Romeo and Juliet* is the effectiveness with which the poetry communicates, and does so when delivered at great speed. Leonardo diCaprio did not slow down in order to get a complex point across. He simply made sure that *he* understood the point and assumed that his understanding would be enough to carry the audience with him. This is what any actor has to do. When we study Shakespeare on the page, for academic purposes, we may require all kinds of help. Generally, we read him in modern spelling and with modern punctuation. And I like an edition, such as the Arden editions, which gives detailed notes on the same page. But any poetry that is performed – from song lyric to tragic speech – must make its point, as it were, without reference back. We can't, as an audience, ask the actors to repeat themselves, or slow down, or share their notes with us. We must grasp the meaning – or enough of it – in real time. That *Hamlet* still works after 400 years is an extraordinary linguistic and poetic fact.

English poetry extends back around 500 years, and its scope is the scope of the English language. That is to say, when a North American, an Australian, an Indian or a Jamaican writes a poem in English, that poem enters the corpus of English poetry. Of course it may be that the poet in question was intending to contribute to a national school of poetry, was intending to add his or her brick to the edifice of a national effort. But the community of any English poem today is larger than any nation-state. And besides, the geography of poetry is not the same as the geography of nation-states. Welsh poetry is written for Welsh-speakers wherever they may be. It is not written for all citizens of the United Kingdom. A Spanish poetry, written for Spanish-speakers in the United States, would enjoy a community, through language, with Hispanics everywhere. An Amharic poet, writing in Toronto about life on the streets of Toronto, would be writing for Ethiopians – or at least Amharic-speakers – everywhere. And a poet writing in Chinese has the notable advantage of being able to communicate with anyone who understands written Chinese: the community is in the script.

Some people have liked to emphasize the difference between English poetry as written in the United Kingdom and English poetry as written in America. So an anthologist begins: 'This anthology of American poetry will be able to extend its charm only to those who genuinely know the American language – by now a language separate, in accent, intonation, discourse, and lexicon, from English.' This is an absurd exaggeration, as even the anthologist in question seems to concede when she continues in the next sentence: 'But the poems collected here can extend their command to anyone able to read English.'*

What is striking about English poetry is not the barriers to appreciation set up between national cultures, but the broad basis for comprehension and appreciation:

> Ah got pompanos!
> Ah got catfish!
> Ah got buffaloes!

---

* *The Faber Book of Contemporary American Poetry*, edited by Helen Vendler (1986), p. 1.

Ah got um!
Ah got um!

Ah got stringbeans!
Ah got cabbage!
Ah got collared greens!
Ah got um!
Ah got um!

Ah got honeydew!
Ah got can'lopes!
Ah got watermelons!
Ah got um!
Ah got um!

Ah got fish!
Ah got fruits!
Ah got veg, yes 'ndeed!
Ah got any kind o' vittles,
Ah got anything yo' need!

Ah'm de Ah-Got-Um Man!

(*The Book of Negro Folklore*, edited by Langston Hughes
and Arna Bontemps, New York 1958, p. 418)

The admirably cooperative, positive, not to say optimistic
attitude of the Ah-Got-Um Man appeals at once to the
imagination, and reminds us of the European poets' and
composers' delight in street vendors' cries. It suggests to me
as well that poetry itself begins in those situations where the
voice has to be raised: the hawker has to make himself heard
above the market hubbub, the knife-grinder has to call the
cook out into the street, the storyteller has to address a whole
village, the bard must command the admiration of the court.

The voice has to be raised. And it is raised in rhythm, as in those highly suggestive work-songs from the American South:

> Well she ask me – hunh –
> In de parlor – hunh;
> And she cooled me – hunh –
> With her fan – hunh;
> An' she whispered – hunh –
> To her mother – hunh:
> 'Mama, I love dat – hunh
> Dark-eyed man' – hunh.
>
> Well I ask her – hunh –
> Mother for her – hunh;
> And she said she – hunh
> Was too young – hunh;
> Lord, I wish I'd – hunh –
> Never seen her – hunh;
> And I wish she'd – hunh –
> Never been born – hunh.
>
> Well I led her – hunh –
> To de altar – hunh;
> And de preacher – hunh –
> Give his command – hunh –
> And she swore by – hunh –
> God that made her – hunh;
> That she'd never – hunh –
> Love another man – hunh.

(*The Book of Negro Folklore*, p. 408)

The last 'hunh', the last stroke of the hammer, is eloquent: the young bride has been unfaithful. And that is why the singer, the poet, is in trouble. That, we understand, is why he is working in a gang. He raises his voice to coordinate the work, and the song he sings can be expected to command the attention and the sympathy of his fellows.

2. Where Music and Poetry Divide

The voice is raised, and that is where poetry begins. And even today, in the prolonged aftermath of modernism, in places where 'open form' or free verse is the orthodoxy, you will find a memory of that raising of the voice in the phrase 'heightened speech'. Poetry is language to which a special emphasis has been given, whether by paring it down and arranging it pleasingly on the page, in lines whose length may be baffling to all but the poet, or by the traditional means which include:

raising the voice in order to be heard above the crowd;
raising the voice in order to demonstrate its beauty and power;
chanting the words;
reciting the words rhythmically;
punctuating the units of speech (what will become the lines of the poem) with rhymes;
setting the words to tunes;
setting the words to tunes and singing them in unison, as in a drinking song.

Some decades ago, it was considered bad form, in the world of poetry readings, to do anything that smacked of *performance*. That poets had once performed their works, chanting them in a manner which approached the bardic, was very much held against them. It was showing off. It was inauthentic. It went out with Yeats and Dylan Thomas.

One night I found myself reading at a technical college, next door to a rugby club dinner. There was nothing for it but to raise the voice, to raise it as loud as I dared. Competing with a drinking song, I turned what I had imagined to be a meditative poem into a full-volume declaration of identity: this is who I am, I seemed to be saying; here I stand, I can no other! Somewhat, but only somewhat, to my horror, the poem appeared to go down very well. I was no stranger to showing off, but I would never normally have shown off in that particular way. One read, or one recited, in the way Auden recited his poems: the proper style was self-deflation.

Since then, I have visited countries in which very few of our assumptions about poetry are shared. I remember a Cambodian picking up my copy of Larkin's anthology of English poetry, and chanting a few pages to himself, uncomprehendingly – because there was to him no other way of rendering a line of verse than by chanting out loud. In Borneo, I was lucky enough to hear a contest of improvised song, which went on through the night. In the Philippines, I knew an illiterate man who had the gift for extempore verse in the traditional Tagalog form, and I paid attention to the way he raised his voice to an appropriate pitch for eloquence.

Some of my educated Filipino friends were aspiring poets, but their aspirations were all in the direction of the United States. They had no desire to learn from the bardic tradition that continued in the barrios. Their ideal would have been to write something that would get them to Iowa, where they would study creative writing. My friends thought of themselves as nationalists, but they did not seem to connect their nationalism with their native poetic traditions. Of course they knew about these traditions, but they probably felt that they could not compete on that ground. Whereas my uneducated, indeed illiterate friend, to whom the word Iowa meant nothing, had a living part in his own tradition, because it was oral and not literary.

Around the same time, I came into close contact with some aspiring American poets – not far from Iowa – and noted in them a familiar negativity in their attitude towards poetic tradition. They felt, in some degree, antipathetic to any poetry not contemporary, and they seemed only to recognize contemporary poetry through a set of negative definitions: it did not rhyme, it did not use metre, it was not interested in form other than what was called 'open form', which was understood to be, when it came down to it, no form at all. 'Heightened speech' was the mantra these poets used, when cornered, to distinguish poetry from prose, but their heightening could not include specifically poetic words, or archaisms, or the special tricks of grammar poets have used in the past.

Most striking to me was the fact that these American poets had a range of tastes in music, and therefore in the lyrics to music, which bore no relation at all to their taste in poetry. It was as if there was a separate part of their brain which dealt with these matters. What is more, in that separate part of the brain, things were really much clearer than in the poetic part. In the musical part of their brains they knew very well what they liked and wanted to hear, and wanted to imitate if they, for instance, were to pick up a guitar and play a tune, or even compose a song. Whereas in the poetic part, their judgements were defensive and somewhat nervous. There was clarity on one side, confusion on the other.

It occurred to me that these poets would be happier if they broke down the barriers in their own brains, if they accepted that the person who was studying creative writing, with the aim of producing poetry, was the same person who had a car full of country and western tapes, or whatever the music was that delighted them. The person who tolerated bad lines in a song lyric was the same person who would tolerate no rhymes at all in a poem. The taste that delighted in the rhythms of rap belonged to the same owner as the taste that had banished metre from poetry.

And there was another notable thing about these aspiring poets, when seen in action in front of an audience – it was quite clear that they would have liked to *perform* for the pleasure of the audience, but that they were hampered by the fact that what they were reading out had been written for the page. They knew this, with one part of the brain, for they asserted, under pressure of questioning, that modern poetry, properly understood, *was* written for the eye, rather than the ear. Whatever 'heightening' it involved, or whatever they did to increase its specific gravity, aural considerations did not enter. But when they stood up in front of an audience, often they would seek to provide some kind of extra interest by making up for what was lacking in the text. And how often one hears even successful and respected poets doing the same. They read to the audience in a manner that is designed to convey *what the poem looks like on the page*, since, truth to tell, the poem was written to look well, not to sound well.

But these poets also would be happier, it occurred to me, if they – even without going so far as to change their basic poetic practice – did themselves a favour and wrote *something*, a single poem even, which they could perform. So that, after the agony of standing in front of an audience reading words which were *specifically designed not to be read out loud*, they could, before leaving the podium, cheer everyone up with something worth listening to.

Now you might ask how it came about that these poets ever even considered mounting the podium, since the precepts of their art militated against it. The answer is that they had probably never really thought through the consequences of their poetic practice, which, as I said, was to proceed by a series of negative definitions: no rhyme, no metre, et cetera. Sometimes, however, I think that poets make no connection between what they do when writing and what happens at a reading.

This may seem implausible, but I shall never forget a confrontation at an international poetry festival between an African and an American poet. The African poet had brought musical instruments with him. He sang and accompanied himself, extemporizing on themes which he, in between times, would explain to the audience. The American was one of those who 'wrote for the page', and over dinner one night he decided to tell the African poet how inconsiderate his kind of performance was. You don't realize, he said, how difficult you make it for the person who reads after you, when you sing your songs and play those instruments. The accusation was that he got the audience into a mood that was prejudicial against the type of poetry he himself had to offer – which he implied was the mainstream poetry (at least as far as the festival was concerned).

The African replied in terms which surprised me at first. You American poets, he said, and you European poets, you think that because you are poets you are very important, whereas I am an African, and I don't think I am important at all. When I go into a village and begin to tell a story, the first thing the audience will do is interrupt me. They will ask questions about the story I am telling, and if I do not work hard they will take over the story and tell it among themselves. I have to work to get the story back from them.

What had struck me as overweening in the American poet – his view that, because his poetry had only limited appeal, other poets should rein in their own performances so as not to show him up – was, to the African, only part of the story.

We all assumed that, because we were poets, the audience would listen to us in appreciative silence. A hush would fall when we approached the rostrum, and when we sat down there would be applause. But to the African these seemed arrogant assumptions. To him, every scrap of attention and appreciation had to be worked for.

In the long run, however polite the audiences have been to our faces, the African poet is right: every scrap of attention and appreciation has to be fought for. A text may be written for the page. Or the written words may be no more than a notation for a performance. But even the most docile of audiences will feel, in the end, that we have overdrawn on its goodwill if we do not ensure we deserve the attention we demand. What the African poet knew within seconds of standing up, we will assuredly learn in due course. We will learn whether we deserve to be heard.

3. The Training of the Poet

One problem we face, as aspiring poets, comes from the lack of any agreed sense of how we should be working in order to train ourselves to write poetry. The old joke – 'Can you play the violin?' 'I don't know – I've never tried' – depends on an understanding of a state of affairs that many a poet might find enviable: there is agreement as to what training and practice might be.

We know, of course, that we will never play the violin on the basis of inspiration alone, and we know that we are unlikely to work out the technique for ourselves, based on first principles. We know we need training and we know we need practice. Whichever direction our efforts lead us in, whether it is the concert hall or the gypsy band, we will know whether we come to be able to do what our peers or our mentors can do.

Supposing that we rise to the heights of our musical profession, we may reach a point when we cannot know for certain, because such things cannot be known by any artist, whether we are merely very good, or whether we have secured a truly distinguished place in the history of violin-playing. But, unless we are engaged in some gross and elaborate form of self-deception, we will know roughly what bracket we belong in.

In the writing of poetry we never know anything for sure. We will never know if we have 'trained' or 'practised' enough. We will never be able to say that we have reached Grade Eight, or that we have left the grades behind and are now embarked on an advanced training. We cannot hop on a train to Paris, or a flight to New York, and go and show our works to an acknowledged master, and ask to be taken on as a student.

There *are* courses in creative writing, and some of these courses are taught by distinguished poets, and it may well suit some temperaments to sign on for the tuition. But to pretend that such teachers are the equivalent of, say, voice coaches would be foolish. It would be very surprising to find a serious opera singer who had not been coached. It would be very surprising to find a poet of whom one could say: she was coached by X, in the way that Callas was coached by Tullio Serafin.

For the poet, there is no equivalent of tuition, and there is no equivalent to the practising of scales or other finger exercises. How comforting it would be if there were, for then we would know about ourselves that we were working appropriately at our task. We could say: is there a quiet room where I can practise? I'll need to put in a couple of hours after lunch. We could reassure ourselves that we were keeping to a disciplined regime, or we could reproach ourselves with the opposite.

But there is no such regime, and any talk of one is best taken as an expression of personal preference. To have a favourite desk in a favourite room would be pleasant, and if the desk had to be entirely clear, save for a supply of blank paper and a pen, that too would be comprehensible. Equally we could imagine such a set up to be inhibiting: we would feel reproached whenever we came anywhere near. A battered old notebook and a knee to rest it on, a stub of an old pencil and a seat in a quiet corner of the bar: that too could be idyllic.

Now when I say that for us, as aspiring poets, there is no such thing as the practising of scales or five-finger exercises, no such thing as sketching from the model, I am aware that the worried reader may object: what about the learning of poetic metres and forms? What about writing sonnets and sestinas and villanelles? Surely that counts as practice.

I don't want my reply to be misunderstood. There is no objection to the proposal: in order to learn to be a poet, I shall try to write a sonnet. But the thing you must try to write, when you do so, is a real sonnet, and not a 'practice sonnet'. Throughout this book, in giving examples of metres and forms, I have tried to use examples of real poems, real lines of verse, not meaningless or flippant 'demonstration models'.

The reason is that a skilful versifier can construct a demonstration model of a complex form, and the thing can be metrically perfect and conform to all the rules laid down, but if we have to excuse it from having any meaning or any artistic value, it becomes a worthless model for us as poets. What the model teaches us is how to write meaninglessly. If the model is flippant, as they often are, it only teaches flippancy.

There is a difference here between, say, a Czerny exercise in music, and the use of poetic models for practice. The Czerny exercise has no pretensions to artistic value, only a technical usefulness. On the other hand, a Czerny exercise does not offend our notion of serious art, since *what it is saying is not silly*.

A trivial model is most likely to point the reader in the direction of triviality. W. E. Henley's 'Villanelle' makes it clear what he thought the limits were:

> A dainty thing's the Villanelle.
>   Sly, musical, a jewel in rhyme,
> It serves its purpose passing well.
>
> A double-clappered silver bell
>   That must be made to clink in chime,
> A dainty thing's the Villanelle;

And if you wish to flute a spell,
　Or ask a meeting 'neath the lime,
It serves its purpose passing well.

You must not ask of it the swell
　Of organs grandiose and sublime –
A dainty thing's the Villanelle;

And, filled with sweetness, as a shell
　Is filled with sound, and launched in time,
It serves its purpose passing well.

Still fair to see and good to smell
　As in the quaintness of its prime,
A dainty thing's the Villanelle,
It serves its purpose passing well.

The poem consciously advises you not to be too ambitious with the form, which it suggests is no longer in its prime, but which will, perhaps, produce something rather sweet.

To get from here to Dylan Thomas's 'Do Not Go Gentle Into That Good Night' might seem impossible:

Do not go gentle into that good night,
Old Age should burn and rave at close of day;
Rage, rage against the dying of the light.

Though wise men at their end know dark is right,
Because their words had forked no lightning they
Do not go gentle into that good night.

Good men, the last wave by, crying how bright
Their frail deeds might have danced in a green bay,
Rage, rage against the dying of the light.

Wild men who caught and sang the sun in flight,
And learn, too late, they grieved it on its way,
Do not go gentle into that good night.

Grave men, near death, who see with blinding sight
Blind eyes could blaze like meteors and be gay,
Rage, rage against the dying of the light.

And you, my father, there on the sad height,
Curse, bless, me now with your fierce tears, I pray.
Do not go gentle into that good night.
Rage, rage against the dying of the light.

You may like this or not. You may feel that it is over-rhetorical and unclear in its thought, that it has too much of 'the swell/ Of organs grandiose and sublime', or you may be moved by it. Whichever reaction you have, the likelihood is that if you start from Thomas's villanelle as a model, you will be setting your sights much higher than if you start from Henley. If Thomas learnt from Henley, it would only have been to ignore his example.

Thomas's father was dying but did not know it, and his son wrote the poem in order to express intense feelings that he could not communicate to his father without letting him know that he was dying. That he should try to express such feelings in the most difficult and intractable of fixed forms (in which the poet must repeat certain lines at given points, as well as follow the set rhyme-scheme) is a point to ponder.

In the latter part of the nineteenth century there was a craze for metrical experiments which introduced or reintroduced several old French and Italian forms to English and American practice. The intricacy of these fixed forms appealed to all kinds of people who liked to fiddle with words. There were ballades, chants royal, kyrielles, pantoums, rondeaux, rondels,

rondeaux redoublés, Sicilian octaves, roundels, sestinas, trio-
lets, villanelles and virelais to play with, and poets of varying
merit had a go. The fascination of Provençal poetry for Ezra
Pound comes out of this mostly unpromising milieu, and it is
interesting that Pound should have been in the end one of
those most associated with the complete upheaval in poetic
practice that constituted modernism.

Among those today who believe that modern poetry *must*
do without rhyme or metre, there is an assumption that the
alternative to free verse is a crash course in villanelles, sestinas
and other such fixed forms. But most of those mentioned in
the previous paragraph are rare in English poetry. Few poets
have written a villanelle worth reading, or indeed regret not
having done so. Thomas's distinction, at the very least, was to
write a villanelle from which both the repeated lines (which
can so often pall with repetition) have entered the language.

That is some achievement. But, for poets today or in any
age, the choice is not between freedom on the one hand and
abstruse French forms on the other. The choice is between
the nullity and vanity of our first efforts, and the developing
of a sense of idiom, form, structure, metre, rhythm, line – all
the fundamental characteristics of this verbal art. Of course
our first attempts will be vain. They *will* be vain because they
must be ambitious.

As Constable once said, rob a painter of his conceit and you
might as well hang him. But if it is conceit that gives us the
courage to embark on our poetry, there is time later for the
Critic Within to put our conceit on its mettle, to make it
work hard on our behalf. But the first questions are the simplest
and the starkest: Why *should* we not make the attempt upon
this art? Why should we not put pen to paper?

4. The Sense of Form

Poetry carries its history within it, and it is oral in origin. Its transmission was oral. Its transmission today is still in part oral, because we become acquainted with poetry through nursery rhymes, which we hear before we can read. And we learn an analysis of these rhymes, a beating of rhythm, a fitting of word to pitch, a sense of structure, long before we can read. And for the most part this analysis is itself never expressed, never codified. It is passed on from parent or other teacher to child.

> If I had money as I could spend
> I never would cry old chairs to mend.
> Old chairs to mend! Old chairs to mend!
> I never would cry old chairs to mend.

Who sits down and tells the parent where to place the stresses in the line? The parent of the parent does so. And the rhyme, if it still gets passed on, comes with its information about days gone by, for of course it is a long time since our streets have resounded to pedlars' cries. (But marketplaces still have their barkers, and auctioneers their patter, and there are places in the world where all these traditional practices are still common.)

For the most part, in the reading – and I would say in the writing – of poetry, the handling of rhythm and form is instinctive rather than codified. We think of a line that sounds well, and only later try it out against a template, to see if it actually fits into our schema. Or we start something, and then look at what we have so far, and then we try to repeat, with variations, what we have already done. We write a line, and then try to compose another to match it. Or we compose a whole stanza and then see how many such stanzas we can devise in order to complete the poem. How many, or how few. We feel our way forward.

Take this poem, 'Break, break, break', by Alfred Lord Tennyson, composed in his grief for his friend Arthur Hallam:

> Break, break, break,
>   On thy cold gray stones, O Sea!
> And I would that my tongue could utter
>   The thoughts that arise in me.
>
> O, well for the fisherman's boy,
>   That he shouts with his sister at play!
> O, well for the sailor lad,
>   That he sings in his boat on the bay!
>
> And the stately ships go on
>   To their haven under the hill;
> But O for the touch of a vanished hand,
>   And the sound of a voice that is still!
>
> Break, break, break,
>   At the foot of thy crags, O Sea!
> But the tender grace of a day that is dead
>   Will never come back to me.

This is as clear a case as you could find of a poem whose form grows with its composition. The first line seems to be the *given*, the starting point for the creation of the form. But what kind of a line is it? Three bleak repeated words, three stresses. In classical metrics there is such a foot. It is called a molossus.

But we can be pretty certain that Tennyson was not thinking, 'Why don't I start a poem with something really obscure, like a molossus?' He had this bleak rhythm in his mind, and then he sought a line which would match it.

So he wrote the second line. And actually this line seems to have four stresses, although it can be read as a three-stress line ('On thy *cold* gray *stones*, O *Sea*'). By the time he has finished the first stanza, this is the form he seems to have chosen: a three-stress-per-line stanza of four lines, a quatrain in which the second and fourth lines rhyme. And this is certainly the form of the second stanza, which comes across as a much more regular piece of versification than the first.

But when he reaches the third stanza, and he comes to the third line, he adds what is definitely a fourth stress to the pattern he has created. And he clearly likes the variation thus created, because he repeats it in the last stanza, putting an extra stress into the third line. Tennyson's love for Hallam and his grief at his death were expressed passionately and at length in *In Memoriam* and other poems such as this. And we know independently that the germ of *In Memoriam* was a poem in which Tennyson regretted the chance to touch his friend's hand and to kiss his brow. In this poem, the line that introduces the variation, 'But O for the touch of a vanish'd hand', is also the line that tells us for the first time what the unutterable grief is about. The line varies, it expands, because it suddenly has an extra freight of emotion.

Regularity, in this poem, is not at a premium. Tennyson follows his feelings in creating each line. He follows the music in his head. If you had asked him, at the end of the day, to describe the prosody of the poem to you, he would no doubt have had to think for a moment before he could answer you, not because he was ignorant of the terms, but because he had been writing a poem, not a metrical exercise. At every point, he was exerting his free will. And the outcome of that exertion was the form.

5. The Iambic Pentameter

A line of five feet, each of which is an iamb, that is to say, each of which is a ti-tum. As opposed to a tum-ti.

Ti-tum ti-tum ti-tum ti-tum ti-tum

In fact, if you analyse a passage of blank verse, that is to say poetry written in unrhymed iambic pentameters, you will find very few lines that conform precisely to this pattern:

The woods decay, the woods decay and fall

Nobody could read this line of Tennyson (from 'Tithonus') without reading it metrically, this is to say, placing emphasis on the second, fourth, sixth, eighth and tenth syllables. But while this is an example of a regular iambic pentameter, it is not common, in good poetry, to find such perfect lines, or to find several of them in succession.

The iambic pentameter owes its preeminence in English poetry to its genius for variation. Good blank verse does not sound like a series of identically measured lines. It sounds like a series of subtle variations on the same theme.

The key to the historic success of this line is its being neither too long nor too short. If it were any longer, the reader would have to emphasize the metre a little more, in order to assert control of the line. You can hear this need asserting itself in English poetry written in the longer classical line, the hexameter. You have to assert the metre, otherwise you will get lost.

But if the iambic pentameter is properly written, you shouldn't have any difficulty understanding how it goes. The poet should have written it so that it comes trippingly off the tongue.

Again, if the poetic line is shorter than the ten syllables of the iambic pentameter, what happens is that the metre asserts itself willy-nilly, because there is less room for variation. This is not a *fault* of shorter lines, it is merely a characteristic of them. You may choose a shorter line precisely in order to enjoy this extra degree of assertiveness. But in choosing the more assertive line you have to bear in mind the length of the poem. You have to decide whether you can keep your more assertive line going for more than a page or two.

The iambic pentameter is ideal for a long poem because of this capacity for each variation.

> The woods decay, the woods decay and fall,
> The vapours weep their burthen to the ground

Once again, in the second line of the poem, it would be hard to read the words wrongly. And yet, if you read the words as they feel they should sound, you will automatically skip the emphasis on the eighth syllable. The metrical template – ti–tum ti–tum ti–tum ti–tum ti–tum – would lead you to expect an emphasis on the word 'to':

> The vapours weep their burthen *to* the ground

But that would sound idiotic. So one of the five metrical accents has been dropped. In the next line, by way of further variation, we find that there are six stresses:

> The woods decay, the woods decay and fall,
> The vapours weep their burthen to the ground,
> Man comes and tills the field and lies beneath

You cannot read line three without placing emphasis on both of the first two words – and this is an effect perfectly consonant with the meaning of the poem. Man has arrived on the scene, and has disrupted things by his arrival. 'Man comes' – if you emphasize both words equally, which is what you are being asked to do, you are turning the first foot of the line into what is called a spondee.

> An iamb goes: ti-tum.
> A trochee goes: tum-ti.
> A spondee goes: tum! tum!

But spondees are much rarer than iambs and trochees in English verse, because it normally happens that if you put two words together, or two syllables together, one of them will attract more weight, more emphasis, than the other. In other words, most so-called spondees can be read as either iambs or trochees.

These technical terms – iamb, trochee, spondee – which come to us from classical metrics, are used as a matter of convenience, but they can give a false impression of rigour when we use them in an English context. In English poetry there is no such thing as a regular use of the spondee – it is more like a specific local effect. You couldn't write a whole poem in spondees – you couldn't even write a single line. But you can write immense poems in iambics.

> The woods decay, the woods decay and fall,
> The vapours weep their burthen to the ground,
> Man comes and tills the field and lies beneath,
> And after many a summer dies the swan.

In the fourth line Tennyson could easily have avoided the extra syllable – the line has eleven syllables – by making the summers into a more conventional plural:

> And after many summers dies the swan.

But he does not do this. Clearly he prefers the idiomatic flavour of 'many a'. But there is another point here: the irregularity he has introduced is not a *mistake*. It is another variant, and in this case a very gentle variant, on the basic pattern. You could argue, indeed, that it hardly counts as a variant, since most people would run the last syllable of 'many' together with 'a', making one syllable. They would elide the syllables. They would create an elision.

Once again, having introduced the metrical term, I should like to warn that elision has a much more precise meaning in Latin metrics than it does in an English context. But it is a useful word, so it gets used.

Looking at the line that Tennyson decided on,

> And after many a summer dies the swan.

we note that, for the first time, there is a certain ambiguity as to how it should be delivered. Clearly the words 'summer', 'dies' and 'swan' are important, but how important is the word 'many'? Is Tennyson saying that swans live a long life measured in summers, before dying? Or is he pointing us toward the thought that their deaths come after summer? One could easily imagine a reader placing an emphasis on 'many', and another reader withholding the emphasis before landing on the word 'summer'.

And this second reading would exhibit a sympathy with the way the line is constructed: it pushes the meaning to the second half, so much that we only find out the subject of the sentence when we reach the last word. This withholding of the subject till the end, by inversion of the grammar of the line, contrasts with the previous line of the poem, in which Man, the subject, arrives on the first syllable, disrupting the metrical pattern.

The next lines of the poem introduce a new metrical trick, enjambment, the running on of one line into the next:

> Me only cruel immortality
> Consumes: I wither slowly in thine arms

After four clearly defined end-stopped lines, each with its subject and its verb, we come to a line which has no verb, and which is impossible to construe until we reach the first word of the next line. This dramatic variation, this running together not of syllables but of lines, is particularly appropriate for this key moment in the poem, which introduces a paradox: the speaker of the poem is immortal, but his immortality is consuming him. He will live forever, but will go on getting old forever. This is the story of Tithonus, the subject of the poem.

People are often uncertain whether, when a line is run on like this, the reader should nevertheless pause at the end of the line, *because that is the way it appears on the page*. The answer is that such a poem is primarily written for the ear, whether for the inner ear of the reader or for the ear of the audience. When the poet has run a line together in this way, he is seeking to vary the line length. The meaning resides in the whole sentence, which happens to be more than a line long: 'Me only cruel immortality consumes.'

In principle it is never incorrect to read an enjambed line straight through, without giving any indication of a line break. That is what the poet has permitted, what he has set up to happen. In practice it might be that the reader wishes to make a slight pause, in order to give special emphasis to the word that begins the next line. But if he does this every time a line is enjambed, the point of the enjambment is lost.

> Me only cruel immortality
> Consumes: I wither slowly in thine arms,
> Here at the quiet limit of the world,
> A white-haired shadow roaming like a dream
> The ever-silent spaces of the East,
> Far-folded mists, and gleaming halls of morn.

There is a second enjambment, less pronounced, after the word 'dream'. If you do not run these lines together when reading them out loud, you will confuse the hearer, because the line 'A white-haired shadow roaming like a dream' sounds as if it is complete as a unit (as if the verb 'roaming' is intransitive, which is what it normally is). But the shadow is not just roaming, it is roaming three things: it is roaming spaces, it is roaming mists and it is roaming halls. To be delivered comprehensibly, the three lines must hang together. If they come apart, the passage turns into chunks of meaningless beauty.

I began looking at these lines because I was in search of an example of a regular iambic pentameter (which I found in the first line), and I continued looking at them because of the wealth of variation shown in line after subsequent line. Taken together, these lines constitute a verse paragraph, an informal term but a useful one because it reminds us that the lines of a poem should hold together, and that in blank verse one must think of the larger unit and make one line produce the next, so that the listener wants to hear more. In other kinds of poem, this making you want to hear more, this engine of forward progression, is a function of rhyme.

6. Variations in the Line

The story so far:

The typical unit of English poetry is the iamb, which goes ti-tum.

Put five of these units together and you get a pentameter.

But it rarely happens that the actual individual line corresponds precisely to the pattern: the genius of the line lies in its capacity for variation.

One source of variation is the shifting of metrical accents: most typically a unit, a foot, which we had expected to be an iamb turns out to be a trochee, tum-ti instead of ti-tum.

Another source of variation is the placing of the pauses within the line. Such pauses are often indicated on the page by commas or other punctuation marks.

A pause may be made – this is an important point, distinguishing English from classical metrics – at any point in the line. Or there may be no internal pause at all. Turning my pages of Tennyson at random, looking for examples of this kind of variation, I come to a poem called 'Aylmer's Field' (line 385):

> Fall back upon a name! rest, rot in that!
> Not *keep* it noble, make it nobler? fools,
> With such a vantage-ground for nobleness!

The punctuation makes it very clear that there are pauses within the line after the sixth and seventh syllables in line one, and after the fifth and ninth in line two, while in line three

there are none. The ear picks up and appreciates these variations as the poem proceeds. There is enough regularity to
meet the metrical expectations, and enough variation to stop
those expectations palling.

There is not, in the English iambic pentameter, any regular
system of internal line-breaks: there is no such thing as a formal
caesura, a break, which has to occupy a particular position in
the line. If a line-break is used repeatedly in the same position,
it is in order to create a particular deliberate effect. Or, if it is
inadvertent, it may be a fault in the poem, a sign of the writer's
lack of competence.

A common variation in the line comes from the addition
of a syllable at the end:

> To be, or not to be, that is the question:
> Whether 'tis nobler in the mind to suffer
> The slings and arrows of outrageous fortune,
> Or to take arms against a sea of troubles . . .

Here, surprisingly enough, we find four of these extra last
syllables in the line, four of these feminine endings in a row.
The passage seems to have suffered no harm as a result,
although I would say that, in terms of pure verse-making, it
hasn't received much benefit either. The repetitive variation
did not offend Shakespeare's ear. More important to him was
the deployment of these particular words at the end of each
line. Their meaning took precedence in his mind. The variation was unimportant. But of course to poets other than
Shakespeare, who valued regularity and seemliness in the line
much more highly than he did, these four famous lines with
their successive feminine endings might have seemed sloppily
written.

That second line – 'Whether 'tis nobler in the mind to

suffer' – shows a further standard variation in its first foot, which is obviously trochaic. If you hear someone trying to scan the line by reading it as 'Wheth-*er* 'tis nobler in the mind to suffer', that person is violating the verse. Scansion is not about mispronouncing the language, or torturing it in order to do something it doesn't want to do.

Now this inversion of the first foot is so useful that it is almost worth considering it as part of the basic pattern of the line, that it can have either an iamb or a trochee at the beginning. The variation is useful because there are many basic words with which we would like to begin a line of verse, but which are obviously trochaic in character: a word like 'never', for instance. The pattern of the line, the potency of the iambic measure, is so strong that it can carry this variation without confusing the listener.

The second foot in the line, on the other hand, is less often tampered with. This is particularly so if the first foot has been inverted to a trochee. If you started the iambic pentameter, irregularly, with *two* trochees in succession, you would probably make it too hard for the mind to construe. (King Lear's line of five trochees, 'Never never never never never', is impossible to read as anything like an iambic line. Lear drops the metre in his grief.)

If we now count up the variations so far enumerated and considered as legitimate (by which I mean only that the ear can comprehend them as variations), we will find that we have already allowed for an astonishing number of line patterns. We have encountered:

1. the basic iambic pentameter pattern;
2. the same pattern with an unaccented extra syllable at the end;
3. the basic pattern but with a trochee in the first foot;

4. the basic pattern but with a spondee in the first foot ('Man comes and tills the field and lies beneath'),

5. any of these patterns, with marked pauses or caesuras occurring at any point in the line, in any number of combinations.

In fact we have implied still more possibilities than this list contains, because we have accepted that extra syllables might be slipped in, and that some of the accents laid down in the scheme may be dropped or transposed. All in all, this looks like a very licentious form of scansion. And there is a further principle of variation still to be discussed.

7. Patterns of Stress

The way we stress a word, in normal conversation, is by leaning upon *one* of its syllables:

Me only cruel immortality

This line has four natural conversational stresses at most, three if you decide not to stress the word 'only'. It has only four stresses because it gives no further opportunity for a stress, because it only contains four words, one of which has five syllables. When we stress the word 'immortality' we do so by leaning with extra weight into the syllable 'al'.

The longer the words in a pentameter, the fewer opportunities for making one of these stresses. One could imagine an iambic pentameter consisting of one word:

Deuterohermeneuticality.

I'm pushing it a bit, but if this word meant anything it would receive one natural conversational stress (one would lean on the first syllable, I presume).

Stress, in this sense, is always linked to meaning. Some words really don't mean very much at all, on their own. They are essential connectors of meaningful words, one to another. Of, and, but, the, which . . . no vivid thought comes to us as the eye travels over these words. But how important they are when we arrange our words in the line, deploying our great units of meaning, our vivid nouns, adjectives and verbs. They are the settings for our meaning-words, always varying the positions of the words we are going to stress. And these stress-words themselves will vary in number. Perhaps it is hard to imagine an iambic pentameter with only one stress, but only two stresses is perfectly feasible:

In Massachusetts, in Virginia

(Robert Frost, 'The Gift Outright') is a conventional iambic line.

As to the maximum number of stresses possible in the pentameter, consider the speech of Lucianus, the poisoner, in the play-within-the-play in *Hamlet*:

Thoughts black, hands apt, drugs fit, and time agreeing,
Confederate season, else no creature seeing,
Thou mixture rank, of midnight weeds collected,
With Hecate's ban thrice blasted, thrice infected,
Thy natural magic and dire property
On wholesome life usurps immediately.

This is sometimes thought to be a speech Hamlet himself has inserted into the play, as part of his plot to prove the guilt of the king. It is in rhyming couplets, each with a feminine ending. The first line is exceedingly dramatic and sinister, and if you saw it by itself you might be hard pressed to be certain what sort of line it was, since every one of the first six words is emphasized. It is a line with eight natural stresses, a line of quite exceptional metrical character. I am always cautious about identifying an English foot as a spondee (see above), but here are three undoubted spondees in a row. Imagine an actor wishing to emphasize the fact that not only are all preparations in order but it is also, most fortunately, the right time for the deed to be done. Conceivably he could stress the antepenulti-mate word:

Thoughts black, hands apt, drugs fit, *and* time agreeing,

in which case we would have a nine-stress line.

But that's really the limit. Much more often, if you count the number of stresses in an iambic pentameter, you will find that there are four, and this is particularly likely in the most regular-minded of our poets, such as Dryden:

> In pious times, e'r Priest-craft did begin,
> Before *Polygamy* was made a sin;
> When man, on many, multiply'd his kind,
> E'r one to one was, cursedly, confind:
> When Nature prompted, and no law deny'd
> Promiscuous use of Concubine and Bride;
> Then, *Israel's* Monarch, after Heaven's own heart,
> His vigorous warmth did, variously, impart
> To Wives and Slaves: And, wide as his Command,
> Scatter'd his Maker's Image through the Land.

> (*Absalom and Achitophel*, lines 1–10)

No feminine endings, very little enjambment, perfect rhymes to mark the couplets – a beautiful balance between scabrous wit and decorum, and a tremendous forward thrust imparted to the passage by the trick of having one sentence continue through ten lines: these are heroic couplets at their most elegant and characteristic. The final syllable of each line is invariably stressed, because it is a rhyme-word. The first foot in each line is almost always a straightforward iamb as well – only the last line of the passage commences with a trochee. So the control exerted over the metre is exceedingly marked. And yet there is no sense of mechanical repetition of a pattern. Dryden has quite enough opportunities for variation.

8. Mysteries of the Trochee

The iambic line, with its characteristic forward movement from short to long, or light to heavy, or unstressed to stressed, is the quintessential measure of English verse. It has its own special genius at four feet, that is in the iambic tetrameter, which being shorter has significantly less scope for variation. At five feet, in the pentameter, it is at its most brilliant. At six feet it is known as the alexandrine, but the alexandrine, although it is the classic line in French poetry, is a poor thing in English. One cannot make whole poems out of it. You can include an alexandrine in a verse-pattern, a stanza in which lines have different lengths. But it is very noticeable that many alexandrines, for instance those used by Edmund Spenser as the last line in each stanza of *The Faerie Queene*, turn out to contain one otiose word.

I used to know a woman of some pretension who liked to exclaim: 'The marvellous French alexandrine, with the caesura in the middle! They tried to do it in English and they couldn't!' This is quite true. At twelve syllables or six feet, the English line begins to break into two, and it is hard to think of an example of a good alexandrine in English, let alone a poem with many marvellous alexandrines. But this should not be a cause for mourning.

When we turn to the trochee, we might expect that it too would furnish us with a handy line five feet long. In fact it has not done so, although the line is theoretically perfectly possible to achieve. It is rare, but we have already encountered one example of it, in the line from a Campion song quoted in the first chapter:

> Followe thy faire sunne, unhappy shaddowe:

It is far from clear, in fact it is a mystery, why this simple metrical pattern has proved so unhandy.

The shorter, four-foot trochaic tetrameter, by contrast, is very easy to fall into:

> Tum-ti tum-ti, tum-ti tum-ti

I've put a comma in there, to draw attention to what the line definitely wants to do, which is not to split in two like the English alexandrine, but to fall into two balancing parts:

> By the shores of Gitche Gumee,
> By the shining Big-Sea-Water

In Longfellow's *The Song of Hiawatha* the English trochaic tetrameter achieved its greatest popularity, and can be studied with all its virtues and vices. It did have some virtues which suited Longfellow very well. He wanted to convey the impression of an oral poetry, and he chose a measure which he found in a German translation of the Finnish oral epic, the *Kalevala*. Although it does not in fact correspond exactly to the original Finnish measure, the trochaic line proved accommodating to the formulas and repetitions characteristic of oral epic verse (including Homer). The problem is that it proved too facile. Many of the names which Longfellow uses – Hiawatha, Minnehaha, Pau-Puk-Keewis, Mushkodasa and so forth – occupy exactly half a line. If you give Minnehaha her name's translation, Laughing Water, that makes a whole line. The Homeric formulas are not as restricting as this. Phrases such as '*polumetis Odysseus*', the many-wiled Odysseus, '*rhododactylos eos*', rosy-fingered dawn, have their own place in the line, but the line they are part of is longer and more complex.

Longfellow was trying to invent an English metric to suit his subject, and to invent an aesthetic to go with it, one in which repetition was actively encouraged:

> Shawdonasee, fat and lazy,
> Had his dwelling far to southward,
> In the drowsy, dreamy sunshine,
> In the never-ending Summer.
> He it was who sent the wood-birds,
> Sent the robin, the Opechee,
> Sent the bluebird, the Owaissa,
> Sent the Shawshaw, sent the swallow,
> Sent the wild-goose, Wawa, northward,
> Sent the melons and tobacco,
> And the grapes in purple clusters.

> (Part II, 'The Four Winds')

But this soon taxes the patience of the reader, who is never entirely convinced that the inevitable metrical variants are legitimate:

> Sent the melons *and* tobacco,
> *And* the grapes in purple clusters.

Two 'ands' in succession fall upon an accented syllable. Are both accents to be suppressed? Somehow it is hard to remember to do this.

What all this tells us is that metrical patterns are not arbitrary designs taken up by chance or promoted by fashion alone. Some things work well in our language, others work well only for the poet who has adopted them, and others don't work at all. Longfellow's poem had great success in its day, and its metre proved catchy and easily imitated, but every imitation turned into parody.

But that does not mean that the trochee itself is unimportant.

9. The Genius of the Trochee

The trochee in fact is extremely important and fruitful, and one way it is fruitful is in a line that is exactly like Longfellow's but without the final syllable. Its cumbersome technical name is the trochaic tetrameter catalectic, where catalectic means lacking the final syllable. This is the measure of Auden's incomparable 'Lay Your Sleeping Head, My Love', a lullaby which is particularly beautiful for its rhythms, of part of his memorial ode to Yeats, of 'The Fall of Rome' and of this 'Autumn Song':

> Now the leaves are falling fast,
> Nurse's flowers will not last;
> Nurses to the graves are gone,
> And the prams go rolling on.
>
> Whispering neighbours, left and right,
> Pluck us from the real delight;
> And the active hands must freeze
> Lonely on the separate knees.
>
> Dead in hundreds at the back
> Follow wooden on our track,
> Arms raised stiffly to reprove
> In false attitudes of love.
>
> Starving through the leafless wood
> Trolls run scolding for their food;
> And the nightingale is dumb,
> And the angel will not come.

Cold, impossible, ahead
Lifts the mountain's lovely head
Whose white waterfall could bless
Travellers in their last distress.

(original version)

It is amazing the difference the loss of the last syllable makes
to the possibilities of the line. Auden, when he was using this
form, was looking back once again to the Elizabethans. Here
is Shakespeare's famous song from *Cymbeline*:

Fear no more the heat o' th' sun,
　　Nor the furious winter's rages.
Thou thy worldly task hast done,
　　Home art gone and ta'en thy wages.
Golden lads and girls all must,
As chimney-sweepers, come to dust.

Fear no more the frown o' th' great,
　　Thou art past the tyrant's stroke.
Care no more to clothe and eat,
　　To thee the reed is as the oak:
The sceptre, learning, physic, must
All follow this and come to dust.

Fear no more the lightning-flash,
　　Nor th' all-dreaded thunder-stone.
Fear not slander, censure rash.
　　Thou hast finish'd joy and moan.
All lovers young, all lovers must
Consign to thee and come to dust.

No exorciser harm thee!
Nor no witchcraft charm thee!
Ghost unlaid forbear thee!
Nothing ill come near thee!
Quiet consummation have,
And renownèd be thy grave!

The reader who goes through every line of this for its metre will notice that there is a certain amount of variation in the pattern. In the first stanza we have feminine rhymes, 'rages' and 'wages', giving us pure trochaic tetrameters for those two lines. In the last line of that stanza a syllable has been added at the beginning of the line, making it iambic – an effect that is repeated in the last couplet of stanzas two and three. In the last stanza of all, the line has been shortened, until a final couplet that brings us back to the original rhythm.

None of these variations is anything less than harmonious to my ear, but in the eighteenth century a charming poet, William Collins, was moved to rewrite the whole song entirely, and one of the consequences of this radical rewrite was the removal of all the trochaic effects. Indeed it would be hard to recognize the source of the song without Collins's title: 'A Song from Shakespeare's *Cymbeline*. Sung by Guiderius and Arviragus over Fidele, Suppos'd to be dead.'

I

To fair Fidele's grassy Tomb
   Soft Maids, and Village Hinds shall bring
Each op'ning Sweet, of earliest Bloom,
   And rifle all the breathing Spring.

II

No wailing Ghost shall dare appear
   To vex with Shrieks this quiet Grove:
But Shepherd Lads assemble here,
   And melting Virgins own their Love.

III

No wither'd Witch shall here be seen,
   No Goblins lead their nightly Crew:
No Female Fays shall haunt the Green,
   And dress thy Grave with pearly Dew!

IV

The Redbreast oft at Ev'ning Hours
   Shall kindly lend his little Aid:
With hoary Moss, and gather'd Flow'rs,
   To deck the Ground where thou art laid.

V

When howling Winds, and beating Rain,
   In Tempests shake the sylvan Cell:
Or midst the Chace on ev'ry Plain,
   The tender Thought on thee shall dwell.

VI

Each lonely Scene shall thee restore,
For thee the Tear be duly shed:
Belov'd, till Life could charm no more;
And mourn'd, till Pity's self be dead.

This example is given not as a model of a successful reworking of another author's text, but as an illustration of the diverse character of metres. One might think – considering the matter in abstract – that there would not be much difference between basing a poem on a ti-tum rhythm, and organizing it on the basis of tum-ti. It turns out that such choices are not arbitrary at all. The different scansions have their different historical associations, their different aesthetic characters. The roughness of one era's poetic practice may be as offensive to a later reader as the smoothness of another's: Collins may sound wrong to us in the same way that Shakespeare sounded wrong to Collins.

10. The Shorter Lines

A line of verse can consist of one word, indeed of one syllable, although in traditional metrics these one-word lines would usually be part of a stanza pattern in which they share the poem with other lines of varying lengths. In free verse it seems somewhat adolescent to imagine that a word will receive maximum emphasis through being placed alone on the line, and that a column of words so arranged will maintain its expressive force. The first line of the poisoner's speech in *Hamlet*, quoted above, does not seem much enhanced when printed thus:

> Thoughts
> Black,
> Hands
> Apt,
> Drugs
> Fit,
> And
> Time
> Agreeing,

but many a poet has written as if this were an improvement. The contrast, on the other hand, between very short and very long lines in a poem can be arresting. A line of a single foot is called a monometer:

I burn.
I fly.
I yearn.
I die.

This form (a quatrain of iambic monometers) doesn't look very promising, but it does most certainly exist, as does its trochaic equivalent. And in case it seems far too recherché to bother about, here is a poem by Kit Wright called 'George Herbert's Other Self in Africa':

> Thinking another way
> To tilt the prism,
> I vowed to turn to light
> My tenebrism
> And serve not night
> But day.
>
> Surely, I cried, the sieves
> Of love shake slow
> But even. Love subsists
> Though pressed most low:
> As it exists,
> Forgives.
>
> But my stern godlessness
> Rose through the sun,
> Admonished me: Fat heart,
> So starving's fun?
> Whom have they art
> To bless?

> Thereat my false thought froze,
>> Seeing how plain
> The field was where they died,
>> How sealed their pain,
>> And I replied,
>>> God knows.

The last line of each stanza is a monometer, the other indented lines are *dimeters*. The first and third lines are trimeters. The measure is iambic, an imitation of George Herbert.

Add a syllable to the monometer, as in the anapaest, which goes ti-ti-tum, and the possibilities increase:

> Thorough bush,
> Thorough briar,
> Thorough flood,
> Thorough fire.

But I have here misremembered *A Midsummer Night's Dream*, in which these anapaests are arranged two per line, that is in dimeters:

> Over hill, over dale,
>> Thorough bush, thorough briar,
> Over park, over pale,
>> Thorough flood, thorough fire – ★

One may think that a line consisting of two feet could hardly be sustained for any serious purpose. A striking proof to the contrary is offered in the German libretti of Wagner, which tend to deal in a variety of short lines. The lines that Isolde sings over the body of Tristan are for the most part trochaic dimeters:

★ II.i.2–5; 'thorough' is an old way of saying 'through'.

Mild und leise
Wie er lächelt,
Wie das Auge
Hold er öffnet, –
Seht ihr's, Freunde?
Seht ihr's nicht?
Immer lichter
Wie er leuchtet,
Sternumstrahlet
Hoch sich hebt?
Seht ihr's nicht?

How gently and quietly
He smiles,
How fondly
He opens his eyes!
Do you see it, friends?
Don't you see it?
How he shines
Ever brighter,
Soaring on high,
Stars sparkling around him.
Don't you see it?

. . . and so on. The trochaic rhythm of the words imparts its character to the music of the *Liebestod*, and while it is not necessarily true that what works in German poetry should work in English, on this occasion the hint might be worth taking.

Campion had an idea for a metre which, though it has not had any success I know of, seems to me interestingly neglected. It adds another syllable to the trochaic dimeter, and Campion thought that it 'answers our warlick forme of march in similitude of number'.

Raving warre, begot
In the thirstye sands
Of the *Lybian* Iles,
Wasts our emptye fields;
What the greedye rage
Of fell wintrye stormes
Could not turne to spoile,
Fierce *Bellona* now
Hath laid desolate,
Voyd of fruit, or hope.
Th' eger thriftye hinde,
Whose rude toyle reviv'd
Our skie-blasted earth,
Himself is but earth,
Left a skorne to fate
Through seditious armes:
And that soile, alive
Which he duly nurst,
Which him duly fed,
Dead his body feeds:
Yet not all the glebe
His tuffe hands manur'd
Now one turf affords
His poore funerall.
Thus still needy lives,
Thus still needy dyes
Th' unknowne multitude.

He called this the 'Iambick Dimeter, or English march', but added 'call it what you please, for I will not wrangle about names'. I would call it the trochaic trimeter catalectic, though English march is better.

11. The Iambic Tetrameter

The four-foot iambic line is a great device, and has been used by the poet desirous of greater speed, and more emphatic rhythm, than the pentameter provides:

> A dog starv'd at his Master's Gate
> Predicts the ruin of the State.
> A Horse misus'd upon the Road
> Calls to Heaven for Human blood.
> Each outcry from the hunted Hare
> A fibre from the Brain does tear.

Blake's couplets in 'Auguries of Innocence' can each stand alone as a proverb. But there is also a tremendous forward thrust, a piling of assertion upon assertion, of proverb upon proverb, which gives the poem its overall tempo. These are couplets, yes, and no sooner has a rhyme been proposed than its answer comes, and these rhymes are nearly all monosyllables. A mysterious effect is created out of very plain statements.

Blake gave himself greater latitude when he used the same measure in a quatrain in which lines two and four rhyme, as in 'The Mental Traveller', the terrifying poem which begins thus:

> I travel'd thro' a Land of Men,
> A Land of Men & Women too,
> And heard & saw such dreadful things
> As cold Earth wanderers never knew.

For there the Babe is born in joy
That was begotten in dire woe;
Just as we Reap in joy the fruit
Which we in bitter tears did sow.

And if the Babe is born a Boy
He's given to a Woman Old,
Who nails him down upon a rock,
Catches his shrieks in cups of gold.

She binds iron thorns around his head,
She pierces both his hands & feet,
She cuts his heart out at his side
To make it feel both cold & heat.

Her fingers number every Nerve,
Just as a Miser counts his gold;
She lives upon his shrieks & cries,
And she grows young as he grows old.

Till he becomes a bleeding youth,
And she becomes a Virgin bright;
Then he rends up his Manacles
And binds her down for his delight.

He plants himself in all her Nerves,
Just as a Husbandman his mould;
And she becomes his dwelling-place
And Garden, fruitful seventy-fold.

And so it goes on, this astonishing story in which the processes of life suffer such strange reversals.

It is by looking at poems like this, rather than by studying the algebra of metrical treatises, that we learn what a metre, what a measure is capable of, and what its chief virtues are.

When Robert Lowell turned to the iambic tetrameter, something he did with great distinction, he allowed himself a great deal of freedom, and was prepared to move between strikingly regular and irregular lines, as in these opening stanzas from 'Waking Early Sunday Morning', which are arranged in octaves (eight-line stanzas):

> O to break loose, like the chinook
> Salmon jumping and falling back,
> Nosing up to the impossible
> Stone and bone-crushing waterfall –
> Raw-jawed, weak-fleshed there, stopped by ten
> Steps of the roaring ladder, and then
> To clear the top on the last try,
> Alive enough to spawn and die.
>
> Stop, back off. The salmon breaks
> Water, and now my body wakes
> To feel the unpolluted joy
> And criminal leisure of a boy –
> No rainbow smashing a dry fly
> In the white run is free as I,
> Here squatting like a dragon on
> Time's hoard before the day's begun!

The last line of the first stanza – 'alive enough to spawn and die' – is the first completely regular iambic line in the poem. But while the passage I have quoted seems to be getting more regular as it goes along, Lowell in fact keeps switching from regular to irregular and back, keeping the poem hectic and lively.

12. The Longer Lines

At somewhere around ten syllables, the English poetic line is at its most relaxed and manageable. At less than eight syllables the rhythm becomes pronounced and there is less opportunity for variation. At more than ten syllables we enter a new prosodic world, interesting in its way, with many opportunities for variation and with its own kind of insistence. For it often seems that, simply to keep a grip on the mechanics of the line, we have to stress its metre as we recite it or read it:

> Comrades, leave me here a little, while as yet 'tis early morn;
> Leave me here, and when you want me, sound upon the
>   bugle-horn.

> 'Tis the place, and all around it, as of old, the curlews call,
> Dreary gleams about the moorland flying over Locksley Hall;

> Locksley Hall, that in the distance overlooks the sandy tracts,
> And the hollow ocean-ridges roaring into cataracts.

> Many a night from yonder ivied casement, ere I went to rest,
> Did I look on great Orion sloping slowly to the West.

> Many a night I saw the Pleiads, rising thro' the mellow shade,
> Glitter like a swarm of fireflies tangled in a silver braid.

>   (Tennyson, 'Locksley Hall')

This is a trochaic line of eight feet, of which the last is catalectic (to avoid continual feminine endings). Very often it has a caesura in the middle, as for instance at the comma after the word 'Pleiads', or perhaps after the word 'Orion' in the previous line, and so the suspicion might be that the line is really two poetic lines printed as one. But the seventh line ('Many a night from yonder ivied . . .') will not split up in this way. And often in the course of the poem there are lines which go best when read straight through without a break. So it is a genuine long line, that has a genuine natural caesura in the middle. Instantly recognizable as Tennyson's line, it was used effectively by Auden in a poem beginning 'Get there if you can and see the land you once were proud to own'.

These long, highly rhythmic lines are associated in our minds with the Victorians and their delight in reciting poetry. Here is Kipling, using a very old measure called fourteeners:

> We've got the cholerer in camp – it's worse than forty fights;
> We're dyin' in the wilderness the same as Isrulites;
> It's before us, an' be'ind us, an' we cannot get away,
> An' the doctor's just reported we've ten more today!

> ('Cholera Camp')

This iambic line of seven feet could be split into two lines of four and three, the ballad metre or 'ballad-measure', but Kipling presents it convincingly as a single line.

A pattern of four followed by three is found in the ballads of the Australian A. B. 'Banjo' Paterson, but in this example the measure is construed by counting four stressed syllables followed by three; the unstressed syllables can vary in number:

> Now this is the law of the Overland that all in the West obey –
> A man must cover with travelling sheep a six-mile stage a day;
> But this is the law which the drovers make, right easily
>   understood,

They travel their stage where the grass is bad, but they camp
  where the grass is good;
They camp, and they ravage the squatter's grass till never a
  blade remains,
Then they drift away as the white clouds drift on the edge of
  the saltbush plains;
From camp to camp and from run to run they battle it hand to
  hand
For a blade of grass and the right to pass on the track of the
  Overland.

('Saltbush Bill')

Eminent among the longer lines that have been imported
into English practice is the classical hexameter. In Latin this
consisted of five dactyls (tum-ti-ti) followed by a spondee
(tum-tum). In the first four feet, any dactyl could be replaced
by a spondee, but the ending of the line was characteristic and
unaltering: tum-ti-ti tum-tum. The famous mnemonic for
this line, in the days when a classical education was at the
height of its prestige, was: 'Down in a deep, dark dell sat an
old cow munching a beanstalk.' Or the line was represented
thus (—— indicates a long syllable; ‿ a short one; where both
are shown in a position it means either can be used there):

— ‿ ‿ — ‿ ‿ — ‿ ‿ — ‿ ‿ — ‿ ‿ — —

However, the metrical system in Latin, the principle on which
scansion was based, was completely different from that in
English. It is called a quantitative metre. It has all kinds of
fixed rules governing the determination of long and short
syllables, rules which cannot possibly apply to the English
language: for instance, if a vowel is followed by two consonants

the syllable is long. The rules for elision are also fixed, whereas in English there are no hard and fast rules about elision. In Latin any word terminating in -am, -em, -im, -om or -um, if it comes before a word beginning with a vowel, will be elided. It is impossible to imagine such rules being observed in English, except by freaks.

It follows that the Latin hexameter, when used in English, has to adapt itself to the English accentual metre, something it has never done successfully in my view. Perhaps the various experiments seemed better when there was an audience who had the classical template in mind.

When a Latin hexameter is followed by a pentameter, the result is an elegiac couplet. This was the standard mnemonic:

> Down in a deep, dark dell sat an old cow munching a beanstalk.
> Out of its mouth came forth yesterday's dinner and tea.

And here is the opening passage of *Amours de Voyage* by Arthur Hugh Clough (1819–61), a poem written mostly in hexameters, but which includes passages in elegiac couplets:

> Over the great windy waters, and over the clear-crested
> summits,
> Unto the sun and the sky, and unto the perfecter earth,
> Come, let us go, – to a land wherein gods of the old time
> wandered,
> Where every breath even now changes to ether divine.

> (Canto I)

The problem with this kind of line is that the highly assertive metre wants to drag it in the direction of the public recital or music hall – in the direction of Banjo Paterson. But that is not at all what Clough had in mind.

Very few of the classical feet, the units of metre, have found a home in English, beyond the world of conscious metrical experiment. Very few classical stanzas have made convincing English equivalents. An exception might be made in the case of Sapphics (see the Glossary for an example).

13. The Shorter Stanza

The Italian word *stanza* means a room, and a room is a good way to conceive of a stanza. A room, generally speaking, is sufficient for its own purposes, but it does not constitute a house. A stanza has the same sense of containment, without being complete or independent. A poem with grandly conceived and executed stanzas, such as one of Keats's odes, should be like an enfilade of rooms in a palace: one proceeds, with eager anticipation, from room to room.

I don't see that a single line can constitute a stanza, although it can constitute a whole poem:

> See the spring. Ling lifts and is a bee.

This single-line poem by John Fuller has an internal rhyme scheme of a–b–b–a.

A couplet, a grouping of two lines, can either stand by itself, as do so many epigrams, or be a constituent part of a poem. Standing by itself, such a poem *may* be called a distich. But a couplet is very often a vehicle for a continuous argument or narrative.

A triplet or tercet is a group of three lines. The term tercet is used specifically for the three-line unit of terza rima, Dante's form in *The Divine Comedy*. Because these tercets are rhymed so as to interlock, I find it hard to think of a tercet as a stanza. The rhymes go like this: a–b–a, b–c–b, c–d–c, and so forth, until the passage ends on a couplet. Whenever in English poetry three rhyme-words are needed, there are problems,

and there are problems with terza rima because it is so associated with Dante, and therefore not likely to be funny. When
it is done well, it can be beautiful. T. S. Eliot, who did much
to encourage the appreciation of Dante as a poetic model, has
a Dantesque passage in 'Little Gidding'. Seamus Heaney, in
the seventh section of 'Station Island', and in a version of
the Ugolino passage from 'Inferno', also imitates terza rima.
Neither poet, however, follows a strict rhyme-scheme. They
go for the feel of the thing, recognizing that in English the
true rhyme-scheme will be too confining.

At four lines, with the quatrain, we reach the basic stanza
form familiar from a whole range of English poetic practice.
This is the length of the ballad stanza, the verse of a hymn,
and innumerable other kinds of verse. A quatrain can come
unrhymed, in which case it is simply a convenient organizing
principle for the poet's thoughts. Or it can rhyme a-b-a-b; or
the first and third lines can go unrhymed, x-a-x-a (x being the
convention for a non-rhyming word); or, to create a lovely
effect, familiar from Petrarchan sonnets, it can rhyme a-b-b-a.
And there are all kinds of possibilities for line-lengths. Short
and speedy can be good, as in this by George Gascoigne
(1534?–77):

> 'And if I did, what then?
>   Are you aggrieved therefore?
> The sea hath fish for every man,
>   And what would you have more?'
>
> Thus did my mistress once
>   Amaze my mind with doubt;
> And popped a question for the nonce
>   To beat my brains about.

Whereto I thus replied:
        'Each fisherman can wish
That all the seas at every tide
        Were his alone to fish;

'And so did I, in vain;
        But since it may not be,
Let such fish there as find the gain,
        And leave the loss for me.

'And with such luck and loss
        I will content myself,
Till tides of turning time may toss
        Such fishers on the shelf.

'And when they stick on sands,
        That every man may see,
Then will I laugh and clap my hands,
        As they do now at me.'

We come in in the middle of an argument between a man and his lover, and, even if it is hard at first to follow all terms of the argument, what comes across most vividly is the sharp, angry idiom. (The woman is saying: so what if I have a roving eye? The man replies: if that is the way of the world, I'm going to steer clear of love, rather than continue to make myself a laughing-stock.) Note the pattern of lines: trimeter, trimeter, tetrameter, trimeter. The last two lines, taken together, make a fourteener, and that is what they sound like.

A cinquain is a stanza of five lines (one can go through life without hearing the term used in normal conversation), and even so small a thing can give an effect of great grandeur:

Hear the voice of the Bard!
Who Present, Past, & Future, sees;
Whose ears have heard
The Holy Word
That walk'd among the ancient trees,

Calling the lapsed Soul,
And weeping in the evening dew;
That might controll
The starry pole,
And fallen, fallen light renew!

'O Earth, O Earth return!
'Arise from out the dewy grass;
'Night is worn,
'And the morn
'Rises from the slumberous mass.

'Turn away no more;
'Why wilt thou turn away?
'The starry floor,
'The wat'ry shore,
'Is giv'n thee til the break of day.'

This is Blake's introduction to *Songs of Experience*. The stanza looks like a miniature version of some great ode (appropriately enough for a somewhat miniature book), but doesn't sound miniature at all.

The beautiful visual and aural effects created by stanzas with varying line lengths were much loved in the seventeenth century. An interesting example is George Herbert's 'Denial', in which each last line, excepting the concluding one, jars by not rhyming:

When my devotions could not pierce
Thy silent ears;
Then was my heart broken, as was my verse:
My breast was full of fears
And disorder:

My bent thoughts, like a brittle bow,
Did fly asunder:
Each took his way; some would to pleasures go,
Some to the wars and thunder
Of alarms.

As good go any where, they say,
As to benumb
Both knees and heart, in crying night and day,
Come, come, my God, O come,
But no hearing.

O that thou shouldst give dust a tongue
To cry to thee,
And then not hear it crying! all day long
My heart was in my knee,
But no hearing.

Therefore my soul lay out of sight,
Untun'd, unstrung:
My feeble spirit, unable to look right,
Like a nipt blossom, hung
Discontented.

O cheer and tune my heartless breast,
Defer no time;
That so thy favours granting my request,
They and my mind may chime,
And mend my rhyme.

At six lines – a sixain, the old books do say – the possibilities for the stanza increase. We find a verse made by adding a quatrain to a couplet, a-b-a-b-c-c, a grouping which looks very like the latter part, the sestet, of a Shakespearean sonnet. And we find Burns's famous stanza:

> Wee, sleeket, cowran, tim'rous *beastie*,
> O, what a panic's in thy breastie!
> Thou need na start awa sae hasty,
>   Wi' bickering brattle!
> I wad be laith to rin an' chase thee,
>   Wi' murd'ring *pattle*!

The poet is addressing a mouse, 'On turning her up in her Nest, with the Plough'. Four rhyme-words are needed for the longer lines, which makes this a good satirical stanza. Whatever the use, it will always remind us of Burns, just as terza rima will always remind us of Dante.

A seven-line stanza (for which the word septet is sometimes used, although the OED does not register this meaning) would seem to enlarge the possibilities still further. Here is the Dorset dialect poet William Barnes (1801–86) addressing 'The Clote', the waterlily:

> O zummer clote! when the brook's a-glidèn
>   So slow an' smoth down his zedgy bed,
> Upon thy broad leaves so seäfe a-ridèn
>   The water's top wi' thy yollow head,
>   By alder's heads, O,
>   An' bulrush beds, O,
> Thou then dost float, goolden zummer clote!

There must be a vast number of variants of such a disposition of lines, each one capable of yielding its own characteristic movement. And yet one does not see a seven-line stanza used often.

One historically important seven-line stanza is rhyme royal, which was employed by Chaucer in *Troilus and Criseyde*, and by Auden in his 'Letter to Lord Byron'. The latter use comes as a surprise because Auden was imitating Byron's comic manner in *Don Juan*, a poem written in ottava rima. Rhyme royal is rhymed in the following way: a-b-a-b-b-c-c, so its overall effect is very like ottava rima, which is rhymed a-b-a-b-a-b-c-c. The difference between these two stanzas might be a small thing if you were writing in Italian. In English, in a poem of any length, the difference is significant, because rhyme royal relieves the poet of the task of providing two sets of three rhymes in each stanza, as in ottava rima.

In an inflected language such as Italian, a word may rhyme simply because it has the same grammatical form as another, simply because it terminates in *-ato* or *-ando* or *-are* (these are all feminine rhymes). It follows from this that there are innumerable possible rhymes in Italian, and that these rhymes do not necessarily have great significance. In English poetry, with its reliance on masculine rhymes, rhymes themselves are harder to find, and they have a rather higher degree of significance.

In Italian, ottava rima was used without problem as the metre of long romances, because it was easy to find two sets of three rhyme-words. In fact the problem is no greater than with terza rima. In English, Byron found that although it was a taxing business to write long poems in big stanzas, the situation was transformed entirely if the poem was satirical or otherwise absurd: if preposterous rhymes were admitted, things went with a tremendous zip. Just as Eliot and Heaney, when imitating Dante, chose not to copy his rhyme-scheme, so Auden (but rather more surprisingly) chose not to try to rival Byron's ottava rima, but to shave off a line and use rhyme royal instead. In all likelihood, very few people noticed.

For an example of rhyme royal as used by Chaucer, the reader is referred to Chapter 1. Here is the opening of Canto VII of *Don Juan*, to illustrate the way Byron can move from mock-elevated to conversational within his chosen form:

> Oh Love! Oh Glory! What are ye who fly
>   Around us ever, rarely to alight?
> There's not a meteor in the polar sky
>   Of such transcendent and more fleeting flight.
> Chill and chained to cold earth, we lift on high
>   Our eyes in search of either lovely light.
> A thousand and a thousand colours they
> Assume, then leave us on our freezing way.
>
> And such as they are, such my present tale is,
>   A nondescript and ever varying rhyme,
> A versified aurora borealis,
>   Which flashes o'er a waste and icy clime.
> When we know what all are, we must bewail us,
>   But ne'ertheless I hope it is no crime
> To laugh at all things, for I wish to know
> What after all are all things – but a show?
>
> They accuse me – me – the present writer of
>   The present poem of – I know not what –
> A tendency to underrate and scoff
>   At human power and virtue and all that;
> And this they say in language rather rough.
>   Good God! I wonder what they would be at!
> I say no more than has been said in Dante's
> Verse and by Solomon and by Cervantes,

By Swift, by Machiavel, by Rochefoucault,
    By Fenelon, by Luther, and by Plato,
By Tillotson and Wesley and Rousseau,
    Who knew this life was not worth a potato . . .

And so on. Byron's most attractive works, to the modern reader, are those in which we can hear his conversational tone of voice: that is, in his letters and in *Don Juan*.

Here is Auden addressing Byron (in *Letter to Lord Byron*, Part 3):

A poet, swimmer, peer, and man of action,
    – It beats Roy Campbell's record by a mile –
You offer every possible attraction.
    By looking into your poctic style
    And love-life on the chance that both were vile,
Several have earned a decent livelihood,
Whose lives were uncreative but were good.

You've had your packet from the critics, though:
    They grant you warmth of heart, but at your head
Their moral and aesthetic brickbats throw.
    A 'vulgar genius' so George Eliot said,
Which doesn't matter as George Eliot's dead,
But T. S. Eliot, I am sad to find,
Damns you with: 'an uninteresting mind'.

A statement which I must say I'm ashamed at;
    A poet must be judged by his intention,
And serious thought you never said you aimed at.
    I think a serious critic ought to mention
    That one verse style was really your invention,
A style whose meaning does not need a spanner,
You are the master of the airy manner.

Few have caught that airy manner better than Auden.

A stanza of eight lines (as for instance in Marvell's 'The Garden') is called an octave. Sicilian octaves rhyme thus: a-b-a-b-a-b-a-b. A nightmare for the English poet.

14. The Longer Stanza

When there are more than eight lines in a stanza, something very grand is being attempted or achieved. Imagine being Edmund Spenser and setting yourself the task of writing a long poem in a stanza which rhymed thus: a-b-a-b-b-c-b-c-c. That is in every stanza you are going to have to find four b-rhymes, three c-rhymes and two a-rhymes. And, after eight iambic pentameters, the last line is to be an alexandrine. I call it a tall order, but Spenser was undeterred:

> As when a ship, that flyes faire vnder saile,
>   An hidden rocke escaped hath vnwares,
>   That lay in waite her wrack for to bewaile,
>   The Marriner yet halfe amazed stares
>   At perill past, and yet in doubt ne dares
>   To ioy at his foole-happie ouersight:
>   So doubly is distrest twixt ioy and cares
>   The dreadlesse courage of the Elfin knight,
> Hauing escapt so sad ensamples in his sight.

> (*The Faerie Queen*e, Book I Canto VI, 1–9)

And Keats too, always a man of great courage, was undeterred when he used this antique stanza in his antique-sounding romance, 'The Eve of St Agnes':

> St Agnes' Eve – Ah, bitter chill it was!
>   The owl, for all his feathers, was a-cold;

The hare limped trembling through the frozen grass,
And silent was the flock in woolly fold;
Numb were the Beadsman's fingers, while he told
His rosary, and while his frosted breath,
Like pious incense from a censer old,
Seemed taking flight for heaven, without a death,
Past the sweet Virgin's picture, while his prayer he saith.

(lines 1–9)

What is the attraction in doing something so difficult, with such uncertain success? A part of it must be the desire to build up a really large coherent structure. The -old rhymes in the Keats example brace together the larger part of it, while the final couplet has been prepared for by the first -eath rhyme. Everything is interlocked until the couplet, with its characteristic extra foot in the last line, tells you the grand machine is coming to a halt.

This is what rhyme does. In a couplet, the first rhyme is like a question to which the second rhyme is an answer. The first rhyme leaves something in the air, some unanswered business. In most quatrains, space is created between the rhyme that poses the question and the rhyme that gives the answer – it is like a pleasure deferred. A quatrain might have only one pair of rhymes: x-a-x-a. As in Keats's ballad 'La Belle Dame sans Merci':

I see a lily on thy brow,
    With anguish moist and fever-dew,
And on thy cheeks a fading rose
    Fast withereth too.

The rhyme-word when it comes informs us (and it always feels slightly early, because line four is short) that the business of the stanza is over. But the pattern of this stanza offers great freedom of invention, since two of its lines can end with whatever word you please.

A quatrain rhyming alternately (a-b-a-b) locks two sets of expectations together: first you are asked to defer the solution of the a-rhyme, next you are asked to wait a moment before the solution of the b-rhyme, and it was this interlocking of the rhymes that clearly attracted a poet such as Dante or Spenser, so that in terza rima the interlocking is continuous, while in the Spenserian stanza it holds nine lines together. But a stanza may hold together without being interlocked in this way, as Keats demonstrates in his odes:

> My heart aches, and a drowsy numbness pains
>   My sense, as though of hemlock I had drunk,
> Or emptied some dull opiate to the drains
>   One minute past, and Lethe-wards had sunk:
> 'Tis not through envy of thy happy lot,
>   But being too happy in thine happiness –
>   That thou, light-wingèd Dryad of the trees,
>   In some melodious plot
> Of beechen green, and shadows numberless,
>   Singest of summer in full-throated ease.

> ('Ode to a Nightingale')

The first four lines could perfectly well constitute an independent quatrain, while the rhyme-scheme of the last six lines imitates the Petrarchan sonnet (although that short line makes for an interesting variation). But the whole scheme hangs together as a stanza, and indeed, not being so closely interlocked, makes a spacious but not excessively demanding pattern to repeat.

Larkin imitates the design in 'The Whitsun Weddings', but he puts his signature on the form by varying the placing of the short line:

> That Whitsun, I was late getting away:
>   Not till about
> One-twenty on the sunlit Saturday
> Did my three-quarters-empty train pull out,
> All windows down, all cushions hot, all sense
> Of being in a hurry gone. We ran
> Behind the backs of houses, crossed a street
> Of blinding windscreens, smelt the fish-dock; thence
> The river's level drifting breadth began,
> Where sky and Lincolnshire and water meet.

The same rhyme-scheme as the Keats here yields a carefully prepared but relaxed, prosy effect: the urban details, lovingly marshalled, prepare us for the beauty of the rural evocation of the last two lines, and a sudden poeticism: 'Where sky and Lincolnshire and water meet.'

When a poet writes a first stanza like this, its form may be influenced by chance. Larkin's placing of a short line early in the scheme may be something that simply happened in the course of the arrangement of the lines. But once it has happened in that way, in a regular stanzaic poem, the pattern must be repeated, but repeated in a way that is not repetitive. If you look at the short lines in 'The Whitsun Weddings' from a technical point of view, you will find that each is handled in a slightly different way: enjambed with line before or after it, made to stand alone, broken with a comma, and so forth. Each variation seems utterly natural, but each has been prepared for.

No poet is required to write in stanzas, or indeed in regular forms at all. Coleridge's 'Dejection: An Ode' has a rhyme scheme and sequence of long and short lines that goes without regular pattern, following the mood and whim of the poet. Such a form is known as an irregular ode:

> A grief without a pang, void, dark, and drear,
>   A stifled, drowsy, unimpassion'd grief,
>   Which finds no natural outlet, no relief,
>   In word, or sigh, or tear –
> O Lady! in this wan and heartless mood,
> To other thoughts by yonder throstle woo'd,
>   All this long eve, so balmy and serene,
> Have I been gazing on the western sky,
>   And it's peculiar tint of yellow green:
> And still I gaze – and with how blank an eye!
> And those thin clouds above, in flakes and bars,
> That give away their motion to the stars;
> Those stars, that glide behind them or between,
> Now sparkling, now bedimm'd, but always seen;
> Yon crescent Moon, as fix'd as if it grew
> In its own cloudless, starless lake of blue;
> I see them all so excellently fair,
> I see, not feel how beautiful they are!

What we have here is something like a stanza to start with, followed by a passage in couplets. The informality of the effect suggests that in his melancholy Coleridge cannot rise to the demands of a succession of stanzas. He writes as the spirit moves him. But this effect is deliberate and controlled.

One of the longer stanzas was made famous by Pushkin in *Eugene Onegin*. In English it places an unusual obligation on the poet, which is that its masculine and feminine rhymes are required to fall at given positions in the stanza. The line is a tetrameter. This has made it a challenge to translate and to use in English, but two poets have given us stories of their own in this form. John Fuller, in *The Illusionists* (1980), threw in for good measure, in the course of his narrative, a free translation of Rimbaud's sonnet 'Vowels':

> A: swart as Alabama mammas
> Aghast at Arrabel's drama, tar,
> A Madagascan sans pajamas,
> Black mass, and Sagan's dark *cafard*.
> E: perfect teeth, sheets, eggs, tents, cheeses,
> Endless Decembers, new deep freezes.
> I: vivid tiling, prickling hips,
> Lightning in Spring, pink smiling lips.
> U: just cut turf (smug thumbs-up suburb),
> Burst thumb (such pus), bush's plump bud,
> Sputum (lung's mucus), tumulus, cud,
> Fungus, butt's scum, surf's rush, surf's hubbub,
> O: ghosts, ohms (off/on), porno book,
> Photo room's glow or God's cool look.

From this the reader will see that the rhyme-scheme in itself is not taxing (a-b-a-b-c-c-d-d-e-f-f-e-g-g). The taxing thing is to stick to masculine or feminine rhymes as the form dictates.

It would seem that once you get the Pushkin stanza into your head, it is hard to get it out again. Vikram Seth, on completing his verse-novel *The Golden Gate* (1986) in this form, garnished it with an acknowledgments page, a contents page and a dedication all in the same stanza.

15. The Sonnet

At fourteen lines in iambic pentameters, the sonnet is slightly too long to be considered as a stanza, although it is very like the stanza from Keats's nightingale ode examined in the last chapter (the shorter lines of the Pushkin stanza give a different feel); and although a sonnet sequence could have an overarching narrative, a poem made up of sonnets would still feel like a poem made up of poems, rather than stanzas.

The Petrarchan sonnet, which is the sonnet in its classic form, tends to split into two sections, known as octave and sestet. The eight-line octave might also feel like two quatrains. It usually rhymes a-b-b-a-a-b-b-a, after which there may come a pause, with a change of rhyme and a change of mood or subject, with the sestet, which rhymes c-d-e-c-d-e.

In this classic version, of Italian origin, it is a demanding form of poem to write in English, although not so demanding as to be stupid. Many minor variations have been introduced into the pattern, and many successful Petrarchan sonnets have been written. Unusually enough, the simpler form of sonnet preferred by Shakespeare has turned out to be less fruitful as a model.

Milton is the master of the Petrarchan form:

> When I consider how my light is spent,
>   Ere half my days, in this dark world and wide,
>   And that one Talent, which is death to hide,
>   Lodg'd with me useless, though my Soul more bent
> To serve therewith my Maker, and present

My true account, least he returning chide,
Doth God exact day-labour, light deny'd,
I fondly ask; But patience to prevent
That murmur, soon replies, God doth not need
Either man's work or his own gifts, who best
Bear his milde yoak, they serve him best; his State
Is Kingly. Thousands at his bidding speed
And post o're Land and Ocean without rest:
They also serve who only stand and waite.

(Sonnet XVI)

Here the whole fourteen-line sequence is treated as continuous (and the old punctuation makes the sense perhaps a little hard to follow at times). The layout on the page invites us to consider the sonnet as consisting of two quatrains followed by two tercets, and that is what the rhyme-words ask us to hear. But the thought runs continuously through the poem, discouraging any subdivision of it.

The two quatrains rhyme a-b-b-a, a-b-b-a, and this arrangement is known as the enclosed order. It has great abstract beauty and is characteristic of the Petrarchan form, although Petrarch did sometimes use alternating rhymes. The rhyme-scheme for the tercets – c-d-e, c-d-e – is to me the most beautiful, but it is not the one that Milton used most frequently. His most favoured scheme was c-d-c-, d-c-d. Milton was not a purist, and he was happy to end four of his sonnets with a couplet, which we are told Petrarch never does.

In the twentieth century, many poets wrote sonnets, by which I mean poems with a fourteen-line rhyme scheme. There were also attempts to promote a non-rhyming sonnet, which the reader may feel misses the point (like non-rhyming terza rima). Rather different is the experiment which reduces the line-length of the sonnet from the traditional iambic pentameter, while preserving a typical rhyme-scheme. This is an approach favoured by poets such as Paul Muldoon and Christopher Reid. Reid's 'Fly' is a good example of this modern, slimmed-down, sonnet:

> A fat fly fuddles for an exit
> at the window pane.
> Bluntly, stubbornly, it inspects it,
> like a brain
> nonplussed by a seemingly simple sentence
> in a book,
> which the glaze of unduly protracted acquaintance
> has turned to gobbledy gook.
>
> A few inches above where the fly fizzes
> a gap of air
> waits, but this has
> not yet been vouchsafed to the fly.
> Only retreat and a loop or swoop of despair
> Will give it the sky.

One wonders whether this should be called a curtal-sonnet, but the dictionary tells us that the term curtal is to be applied to an animal that has had its tail docked, that is a sonnet short of a number of lines. Gerard Manley Hopkins (1844–89) used this expression to describe two of his poems, 'Peace' and 'Pied Beauty'. Here is the latter:

> Glory be to God for dappled things –
>   For skies of couple-colour as a brinded cow;
>   For rose-moles in all stipple upon trout that swim;
> Fresh-firecoal chestnut-falls; finches' wings;
>   Landscape plotted and pieced – fold, fallow, and plough;
>   And áll trádes, their gear, tackle and trim.

All things counter, original, spare, strange;
  Whatever is fickle, freckled (who knows how?)
   With swift, slow, sweet, sour; adazzle, dim;
He fathers-forth whose beauty is past change:
     Praise him.

Leaving aside the curious accentual markings by which Hopkins attempted to explain his metrical system, the reason why Hopkins thought of this as a kind of sonnet was, as he explained in a preface, that it was 'constructed in proportions resembling those of the sonnet proper' – that is 6:4 lines as opposed to 8:6. But of course the first part of 'Pied Beauty' has the rhyme scheme of the sestet of a sonnet, and that is why it reminds us of one.

It is Shakespeare, preeminently, who ends his sonnets with a couplet. As soon as you do so, you tend to turn the sonnet into a twelve-line poem (of three quatrains normally) to which a final couplet has been added, and this, as Auden points out, can be a snare, so that even in some of the best sonnets 'the couplet lines are the weakest and dullest in the sonnet' and give the reader a sense of anticlimax. But Auden goes on:

Despite all this, it seems to me wise of Shakespeare to have chosen the form he did rather than the Petrarchan. Compared with Italian, English is so poor in rhymes that it is almost impossible to write a Petrarchan sonnet that sounds effortless throughout. In even the best examples from Milton, Wordsworth, Rossetti, for example, one is almost sure to find at least one line the concluding word of which does not seem inevitable, the only word which could accurately express the poet's meaning; one feels it is only there because the rhyme demanded it.*

* Signet Classics edition of Shakespeare's sonnets, p. xxv.

Auden pointed out that the sonnet form Shakespeare used allowed him to create a cumulative effect:

> Tyr'd with all these for restfull death I cry,
> As to behold desert a begger borne,
> And needie Nothing trimd in jollitie,
> And purest faith unhappily forsworne,
> And gilded honor shamefully misplast,
> And maiden vertue rudely strumpeted,
> And right perfection wrongfully disgrac'd,
> And strength by limping sway disabled,
> And arte made tung-tide by authoritie,
> And Folly (Doctor-like) controuling skill,
> And simple-Truth miscalde Simplicitie,
> And captive-good attending Captaine ill.
>
>   Tyr'd with all these, from these would I be gone,
>   Save that to dye, I leave my love alone.

This is Sonnet 66 in the original spelling and punctuation, in an edition edited by Martin Seymour-Smith for Heinemann Educational Books. It is interesting occasionally to read Shakespeare in this way. We seldom see his plays in old spelling. When Auden says that Shakespeare was wise to choose his easier form of the sonnet, he means in part that it was a wise move for one embarking on a considerable sequence of sonnets. But it was not a wisdom that Auden himself followed in his own sonnet sequences.

There is a type of sonnet sequence (there are examples by John Fuller and George Macbeth) in which the last line of the first sonnet forms the first of the second, and the last of the second the first of the third and so on for fourteen sonnets. The first lines of each of the sonnets, taken in order, comprise a fifteenth sonnet, which completes the sequence.

But there are perhaps easier ways of driving yourself mad.

16. Minor Forms

Some forms are simply not serious. There is no such thing as a serious clerihew:

> George the Third
> Ought never to have occurred.
> One can only wonder
> At so grotesque a blunder.

(E. C. Bentley)

To take this seriously would be seriously to miss the point of it. And I doubt there could be such a thing as a serious limerick:

> When Gauguin was visiting Fiji
> He said, 'Things are different here, e.g.
>   While Tahitian skin
>   Calls for tan, spread on thin,
> You must slosh it on here with a squeegee.'

(Robert Conquest)

What the reader or listener wants to know is how the poet is going to come up with the rhymes for Fiji – we do not go to this text for information about Gauguin or his art, or indeed for a witty observation about Gauguin, since the poem isn't *about* him. It is about rhyming.

The double dactyl, with its fascinating rule that the second part should contain a line consisting of one double-dactyl word, is another form that forbids a straight face:

> Higgledy piggledy
> Vladimir Nabokov –
> Wait! Hasn't somebody
> Made a mistake?
>
> Out of such errors, Vla–
> *di*mir Na*bo*kov would
> Sesquipedalian
> Paragraphs make.

(*New Statesman* competition)

I suppose however this has utility as a mnemonic, if one wants to remember how to pronounce the novelist's name. (The form requires that the first line be nonsense words, the second a name, and that the single-word double dactyl appear in the second part.)

Auden thought the triolet was too trivial a form to bother with, as most examples amply prove. But here is Wendy Cope's triolet, 'Valentine':

> My heart has made its mind up
> And I'm afraid it's you.
> Whatever you've got lined up,
> My heart has made its mind up
> And if you can't be signed up
> This year, next year will do.
> My heart has made its mind up
> And I'm afraid it's you.

This gives us a sense of an appropriate idiom for the form.

What restricts the usefulness of a form is not the absolute difficulty of pulling it off once. It is the difficulty of doing it again, and again, and again. John Fuller, in response to a competition challenge, set out to write a poem consisting only of three-letter words. And in order to add to the interest, he decided on a form in which there were three three-letter words per line, and the lines came in groups of three. The resultant poem is extremely beautiful, but it is the *only* beautiful poem in this form. It is called 'The Kiss':

Who are you,
You who may
Die one day,

Who saw the
Fat bee and
The owl fly

And the sad
Ivy put out
One sly arm?

Not the eye,
Not the ear
Can say Yes:

One eye has
Its lid and
Can get shy;

One ear can
Run out and
Off the map;

One eye can
Aim too low
And not hit;

One ear can
Hug the air,
Get too hot.

But lip and
Red lip are
Two and two,

His lip and
Her lip mix
And are wed,

Lip and lip
Can now say:
'You may die

But not yet.
Yes, you die
But not yet.'

The old lie.

The example tells us that a very difficult form (in this case, next to impossible) does not automatically become funny or light. Here the poem is serious or it is nothing.

Some forms are difficult and major (the sonnet is one of these) and some are too specialized in their difficulty to occupy any but a minor part in the great scheme of things. In Chapter 3 I printed two contrasting villanelles, the first of which conceived the form itself to be irremediably minor, the second (by Dylan Thomas) being one of the handful of serious successes in the genre. One must never say that, in order to learn the art or the craft of poetry, it is necessary on the way to master the art of the villanelle. Great poetry does not have to be technically intricate.

Often coupled with the villanelle is the sestina, in which the final words of each line of the first stanza are repeated, in given variations of the sequence, in another five stanzas, before a final three-line envoi, employing the same words in their last combination. Because it is not a rhyming form (although Swinburne and others have tried adding rhyme to the mix), it is not technically difficult to pull off. The awkwardness is in making it interesting.

Two ways have been tried. One uses somewhat inconspicuous words, on which it is easy to improvise variations. Kipling's end-words in the sestina below are of this kind: all, world, good, long, done, die. The other approach takes very noticeable and characterful words, which tax the ingenuity of the poet, but which play to the distinctive strength of the form. Auden, in *The Orators*, wrote a sestina using the end-words country, vats, wood, bay, clock and love. Every time the word 'vats' comes up, you wonder how he's going to handle it. In the example I give, from Elizabeth Bishop, the end-words are similarly noticeable: coffee, crumb, balcony, miracle, sun, river.

Here is Kipling's 'Sestina of the Tramp-Royal':

> Speakin' in general, I 'ave tried 'em all –
> The 'appy roads that take you o'er the world.
> Speakin' in general, I 'ave found them good
> For such as cannot use one bed too long,
> But must get 'ence, the same as I 'ave done,
> An' go observin' matters till they die.
>
> What do it matter where or 'ow we die,
> So long as we've our 'ealth to watch it all –
> The different ways that different things are done,
> An' men an' women lovin' in this world;
> Takin' our chances as they come along,
> An' when they ain't, pretendin' they are good?

In cash or credit – no, it aren't no good;
You 'ave to 'ave the 'abit or you'd die,
Unless you lived your life but one day long,
Nor didn't prophesy nor fret at all,
But drew your tucker some'ow from the world,
An' never bothered what you might ha' done.

But, Gawd, what things are they I 'aven't done?
I've turned my 'and to most, an' turned it good,
In various situations round the world –
For 'im that does not work must surely die;
But that's no reason man should labour all
'Is life on the same shift – life's none so long.

Therefore, from job to job I've moved along.
Pay couldn't 'old me when my time was done,
For something in my 'ead upset me all,
Till I 'ad dropped whatever 'twas for good,
An', out at sea, be'eld the dock-lights die,
An' met my mate – that wind that tramps the world!

It's like a book, I think, this bloomin' world,
Which you can read and care for just so long,
But presently you feel that you will die
Unless you get the page you're readin' done,
An' turn another – likely not so good;
But what you're after is to turn 'em all.

Gawd bless this world! Whatever she 'ath done –
Excep' when awful long – I've found it good.
So write, before I die, ''E liked it all!'

The point in this vernacular poem is to get across a convincing
picture of a personality, or philosophy of life, and to make the
portrayal as natural as possible. Although the title announces

that here is a sestina, the poem conceals its method of construction. The effect of the repetitions is subliminal.

In Bishop's 'A Miracle for Breakfast' naturalness of movement, of progression, is again at a premium, since after all a
story is being told, but the repetitions are noticeable and
contribute to the character of the mystery that unfolds:

> At six o'clock we were waiting for coffee,
> waiting for coffee and the charitable crumb
> that was going to be served from a certain balcony,
> – like kings of old, or like a miracle.
> It was still dark. One foot of the sun
> steadied itself on a long ripple in the river.
>
> The first ferry of the day had just crossed the river.
> It was so cold we hoped that the coffee
> would be very hot, seeing that the sun
> was not going to warm us; and that the crumb
> would be a loaf each, buttered, by a miracle.
> At seven a man stepped out on the balcony.
>
> He stood for a minute alone on the balcony
> looking over our heads toward the river.
> A servant handed him the makings of a miracle,
> consisting of one lone cup of coffee
> and one roll, which he proceeded to crumb,
> his head, so to speak, in the clouds – along with the sun.
>
> Was the man crazy? What under the sun
> was he trying to do, up there on his balcony!
> Each man received one rather hard crumb,
> which some flicked scornfully into the river,
> and, in a cup, one drop of coffee.
> Some of us stood around, waiting for the miracle.

I can tell what I saw next; it was not a miracle.
A beautiful villa stood in the sun
and from its doors came the smell of hot coffee.
In front, a baroque white plaster balcony
added by birds, who nest along the river,
– I saw it with one eye close to the crumb –

and galleries and marble chambers. My crumb
my mansion, made for me by a miracle,
through ages, by insects, birds, and the river
working the stone. Every day, in the sun,
at breakfast time I sit on my balcony
with my feet up, and drink gallons of coffee.

We licked up the crumb and swallowed the coffee.
A window across the river caught the sun
as if the miracle were working, on the wrong balcony.

About this surrealist-sounding poem we know that Bishop, rather surprisingly, said: 'Oh, that's my Depression poem. It was written shortly after the soup-lines and the men selling apples, around 1936 or so. It was my "social consciousness" poem, a poem about hunger.'[*] Marianne Moore, taking the view that the end-words should not rhyme, thought that 'sun' and 'crumb' were too close in sound. Bishop acknowledged this as a fault, during the course of a letter to Moore, in which she also discussed the two approaches to a sestina I mentioned above. Bishop says:

It seems to me there are two ways possible for a sestina – one is to use unusual words as terminations, in which case they would have

---

[*] Interviewed by Ashley Brown in 1966. See *Conversations with Elizabeth Bishop*, ed. George Monteiro (University Press of Mississippi, 1996), p. 25.

to be used differently as often as possible . . . That would lead to a very highly seasoned kind of poem. And the other way is to use as colorless words as possible – like Sydney [*sic*], so that it becomes less of a trick and more of a natural theme and variations. I guess I have tried to do both at once.*

The Sidney referred to is Sir Philip Sidney, whose double sestina is printed by William Empson in his *Seven Types of Ambiguity*, which Bishop had just been reading. What Empson says about Sidney's poem gives us an idea of the effect Bishop might have been seeking in her own work. Sidney's end-words were as follows: mountains, valleys, forests, music, evening, morning. The poem beats, says Empson, 'with a wailing and immovable monotony, for ever upon the same doors in vain'. And:

The form takes its effect by concentrating on these words and slowly building up our interest in them; all their latent implications are brought out by the repetitions; and each in turn is used to build up some simple conceit. So that when the static conception of the complaint has been finally brought into light (I do not mean by this to depreciate the sustained magnificence of its crescendo but to praise the singleness of its idea), a whole succession of feelings about the local scenery, the whole way in which it is taken for granted, has been enlisted into sorrow and beats as a single passion of the mind.

And Empson concludes that 'limited as this form [the double sestina] may be, the capacity to accept a limitation so unflinchingly, the capacity even to conceive so large a form as a unit

* Quoted in *Becoming a Poet: Elizabeth Bishop with Marianne Moore and Robert Lowell* by David Kalstone (Farrar Straus, 1989), p. 49.

of sustained feeling, is one that has been lost since that age'.★
This might be read as a challenge. And we have here evidence
of the transmission of a form from one poet to another. Moore
recommended Bishop to read Empson's book, Empson
praised the (double) sestina. Bishop went on to write her single
version. And John Ashbery, on reading that, was moved to
write his own first sestina, 'The Painter'.

The sequence of end-words in a sestina is as follows:

First Stanza: 1-2-3-4-5-6
Second Stanza: 6-1-5-2-4-3
Third Stanza: 3-6-4-1-2-5
Fourth Stanza: 5-3-2-6-1-4
Fifth Stanza: 4-5-1-3-6-2
Sixth Stanza: 2-4-6-5-3-1
Envoi: First line contains 2 and 5
      Second line contains 4 and 3
      Third line contains 6 and 1

Sidney's double sestina simply repeats the pattern of the first
six stanzas in stanzas seven to twelve, but then has a different
arrangement of words in the envoi.

Envoi: First line contains 1 and 2
      Second line contains 3 and 4
      Third line contains 5 and 6

The fact that we can find villanelles by Auden, Empson and
Thomas, and sestinas by Kipling, Pound, Auden, Bishop and
Ashbery (and many other poets, in both cases) means that they
are English forms – by adoption, as the sonnet is English only

★ *Seven Types of Ambiguity* (Penguin, 1930), p. 59.

by adoption. A large number of other medieval forms allegedly exist, but one is hard put to find good examples of them that are not, when you come down to it, metrical exercises. (I refer to examples of rare forms and metres by such figures as Swinburne and Austin Dobson.)

Also in this context I might mention that the fact that rhymes exist illustrating classical metres such as the dochmiac –

> The pale kangaroos
> Resent leather shoes

– does not mean that those metres have actually been successfully imported into English verse. For the purpose of understanding English poetry, you can forget the dochmiac, and the molossus, and galliambics, and minor ionics and many other things that have names but no actual application.

17. Rhyme

A glance at the history of European poetry is enough to inform us that rhyme itself is not indispensable. Latin poetry in the classical age had no use for it, and the kind of Latin poetry that does rhyme – as for instance the medieval *Carmina Burana* – tends to be somewhat crude stuff in comparison with the classical verse that doesn't. Anglo-Saxon poetry, which worked on altogether different principles from the poetry associated with the modern English language, had no place for rhyme.

For the last five hundred years, however, English poetry has been very closely associated with rhyme, even though rhyme is optional. It would have been hard until recently to imagine a popular song that did not rhyme, just as it would have been hard to imagine an opera with a prose libretto much before Debussy's *Pelléas et Mélisande* (1902). On the other hand it was established very early on that neither epic nor dramatic verse in English need rhyme. Rhyme was associated with the kind of poetry we call lyric.

In the rhyming contest I witnessed in Borneo, the women danced opposite the men, and a soloist on either side sang a rhyming stanza, which the opposing soloist had to devise an answer to. In between each improvised verse there was a set chorus, which gave each soloist a little time to think up the next stanza. The language of the contest was Malay, which is easy to rhyme in, but which was the second language of the participants. The contest went on and on through the night, with many substitutes on the men's side, as their soloists fell exhausted by the wayside, but only one young girl on the women's side, who was unbeatable.

In the Philippines, where debating contests are held in verse, in the Tagalog language, the principle of the rhyme seems different from anything in Europe, so that the last syllable of one line rhymes with the penultimate of the next. English improvisation is hard enough, but it would be impossible to improvise along these lines. Nevertheless, we do find in rap a style of improvised or semi-improvised rhyming verse, which has this ancient quality to it, so that it seems part of a contest – a contest against all comers, perhaps; an assertion of the rap artist's supremacy in his field. Boasting and insulting are two traditional poetic modes.

In rap, as in most popular lyrics, a very low standard is set for rhyme; but this was not always the case with popular music. The rhymes used to be precise (even if not of high quality) or precise *and* of very high comic or witty quality. At a time, for instance, when American poets were eschewing rhyme altogether, the lyricists of Broadway were at their most ingenious and sophisticated.

They went for a precision of effect which might involve far-fetched words, surprising twists of grammar, and all kinds of resort to the vernacular. The wit was in the accuracy of the upshot. Here for instance is Sportin' Life's sermon from Gershwin's *Porgy and Bess*:

> It ain't necessarily so,
> It ain't necessarily so –
> De t'ings dat yo' li'ble
> To read in de Bible –
> It ain't necessarily so.

Li'l David was small, but – oh my!
Li'l David was small, but – oh my!
He fought big Goliath
Who lay down an' dieth –
Li'l David was small, but – oh my!

     Wadoo! Zim bam boddle-oo,
       Zim bam boddle-oo!
     Hoodle ah da wah da!
       Hoodle ah da wah da!
     Scatty wah! Yeah!

Oh Jonah, he lived in de whale,
Oh Jonah, he lived in de whale –
Fo' he made his home in
Dat fish's abdomen –
Oh Jonah, he lived in de whale.

Li'l Moses was found in a stream,
Li'l Moses was found in a stream –
He floated on water
Till Ole Pharaoh's daughter
She fished him, she says, from dat stream.

In ain't necessarily so,
It ain't necessarily so.
Dey tell all you chillun
De debble's a villun
But 'tain't necessarily so.

To get into hebben,
Don't snap fo' a seben –
Live clean! Don't have no fault!
Oh, I takes dat gospel
Whenever it's pos'ple –
But wid a grain of salt!

> Methus'lah live nine hundred years,
> Methus'lah live nine hundred years –
> But who calls dat livin'
> When no gal'll give in
> To no man what's nine hundred years?
>
> I'm preachin' dis sermon to show
> It ain't nessa, ain't nessa,
> Ain't nessa, ain't nessa,
> Ain't necessarily so!

The lyricist asserts that, given the vernacular in question, 'possible' rhymes with 'gospel' and 'liable' with 'Bible'. The assertion has to be simultaneously far-fetched and entirely convincing for the comic effect to work. A Broadway rhyme will often test our tolerance for the far-fetched.

> Use your mentality!
> Wake up to reality!

Nobody says or said 'Use your mentality' in this way, to mean use your brain or use your intelligence. But in the song in question ('I've got you under my skin') the expression works as a slightly florid way of talking, with a certain extra brio.

And note a simple point, with general application: the lyricist on this occasion takes the far-fetched rhyme, which is perhaps in need of protection, and places it first, so that he gives the illusion that the song is working inevitably towards the second rhyme – 'Wake up to reality'. It is often the case that a weak rhyme can be made to look stronger by being placed first.

Generally speaking, rhyme is the marker for the end of a line. The first rhyme-word is like a challenge thrown down, which the poem itself has to respond to. The answering rhyme (in cases where, as most commonly, the rhymes come in pairs) reminds us of the first rhyme. In consequence, a poem that rhymes becomes easier to remember than one that doesn't. Rhyme is a mnemonic device, an aid to the memory. And some poems are themselves mnemonics, that is to say the whole purpose of the poem is to enable us to remember some information.

So if poetry is supposed to be memorable speech, it is worth bearing in mind that rhyme aids its memorability.

A rhyme-pattern in longer stanzas gives us a sense of where we are in the stanza, and how soon we can expect it to end, for the stanza cannot end until all the rhymes have been answered. But there is a limit to the length of time we can keep a rhyme in our head. If the first line of a poem rhymes with the eleventh, and there has been no intervening pointer to this particular rhyme, the reader is not going to get it.

Of course the poet may take the view that this is OK, since the structure of the work is to be invisible and inaudible. That is fine if intended. Dylan Thomas, in the poem called 'Prologue', had a rhyme-scheme that went 1–51 and then 51–1, that is to say that the first line was paired with the last, the second with the penultimate and so on. Around the middle of the poem you might see that this was what the poet had in mind, but if you miss it, you miss it.

The basic rhymes in English are masculine, which is to say that the last syllable of the line is stressed: 'lane' rhymes with 'pain', but it also rhymes with 'urbane' since the last syllable of 'urbane' is stressed. 'Lane' does not rhyme with 'methane'. A perfect rhyme needs the same rhyme-sound, in this case '-ane' matched with a different consonantal prefix. 'Plain' does not correctly rhyme with 'explain', annoying though this may be, nor does 'bane' rhyme with 'urbane', although one could imagine a poem made entirely of such incorrect rhymes, as indeed one could imagine a poem in which the stressed rhyme-syllable had to rhyme with a non-stressed syllable in the next line, as in 'lane' and 'methane'.

With feminine rhymes it is normally the penultimate syllable that is stressed and therefore contains the rhyme-sound: 'dearly' rhymes with 'nearly', but also with 'sincerely' and 'cavalierly'. Mysteriously enough, a perfectly good word like 'cavalierly' is much easier to accommodate into a comic poem as a rhyme-word, than into anything on the solemn side. Feminine rhymes are the bane of translators of Italian opera, because they are continually needed, but it is always easier to think of a comic solution than a serious one. And that is why grand opera sometimes used to sound like operetta when translated into English.

One solution to this problem has been to use half-rhymes, which in the nineteenth century would not have been tolerated, but which have come into poetry and song more and more. Half-rhymes, which in the context of Wilfred Owen's poetry tend to be called pararhymes (a pararhyme is said to have the same consonantal pattern but a different vowel), were introduced as a form of shock tactic, but have remained in use for a quite different reason: poets like using a vague half-rhyme in order to get a faint effect of a rhyme, rather than a straight, up-front, in-your-face, perfect masculine rhyme.

I privately think that if you start a poem in half-rhymes, you should keep strictly to that effect throughout the whole of the poem. But it often happens to one thinking in half-rhymes that irresistible perfect rhymes occur.

'Love' is so short of perfect rhymes that convention allows half-rhymes like 'move'. The alternative is a plague of doves, or a kind of poem in which the poet addresses his adored both as 'love' and as 'guv' – a perfectly decent solution once, but only once, in a while.

18. Syllabics

The most familiar form of syllabic verse is the haiku, borrowed from the Japanese, in which the poem adds up to seventeen syllables divided into three lines of five, seven and five syllables respectively. To me this seems like an oriental tradition which, however enthusiastically adopted (particularly in schools, I find), is unlikely to have an equivalent effect in the West. A bit like the tea ceremony.

The term syllabics is usually used to refer to a kind of poetry in which the principle of organization of the line is by number of syllables *and nothing else.* That is to say, one does not flirt with traditional metres in a syllabic poem – indeed one struggles at times to avoid them – whereas it may be perfectly reasonable, in a certain kind of free verse, to allow iambic rhythms to creep in. In my opinion, it is easier to avoid iambic rhythms, when writing in syllabics, if you create a line or pattern of lines using odd numbers of syllables.

Can the ear hear a thirteen-syllable line as consisting of thirteen syllables? I don't think so, but I think that a series of thirteen-syllable lines (supposing that was the length chosen) would, after a while, begin to have a characteristic resemblance. For the most part, though, counting the syllables seems to be something that works, if it works, for the poet. It is a private method of organization. (Auden once wrote a poem in which the principle of organization was the number of words per line. He was very proud of having thought this up, and sorry that no one noticed.)

Marianne Moore is the great practitioner of syllabic verse.

The first stanza of 'Virginia Britannia' will give an idea of the gorgeous descriptive effects built up in the course of the full twelve stanzas:

> Pale sand edges England's Old
> Dominion. The air is soft, warm, hot
> above the cedar-dotted emerald shore
> known to the red-bird, the red-coated musketeer,
> the trumpet-flower, the cavalier,
> the parson, and the wild parishioner. A deer-
> track in a church-floor
> brick, and a fine pavement tomb with engraved top, remain.
> The now-tremendous vine-encompassed hackberry
> starred with the ivy-flower,
> shades the tall tower;
> And a great sinner lyeth here under the sycamore.

How would you read this poem aloud? Not by trying to emphasize that the syllables have all been counted. The rhymes will gently do the work of marking the line-endings, and I think the reader is entitled to as much enjambment as he or she feels like, since the author has left us a large number of weak line endings in the poem, which ask to be run on.

Note that the line 'above the cedar-dotted emerald shore' reads as an iambic pentameter, although it has eleven syllables. Any poem in syllabics which features an eleven-syllable line will have this problem of approximation, but Moore did not seem to mind. The poem was written to look good on the page, which it does, and to sound well declaimed, although the structure when declaimed is quite different to the one perceived by the eye. No doubt the author had all kinds of other private rules she followed, whose effect is not visible to us. One thinks of parallels in music, where a word has been encrypted into the bass line. You have to be a musicologist to recognize the fact, but it is there nonetheless, as a principle of organization.

19. Free Verse

Consulting the *Oxford Companion to English Literature* (New Edition, 1985) on the subject of metre, we find in the last paragraph that 'Verse in the twentieth century has largely escaped the straitjacket of traditional metrics.' *Verse* has escaped. It is not even a question of *poetry* having escaped, leaving verse (as in light verse) with its arms bound tightly across its chest, in the manner of the traditional straitjacket. Verse escaped. Verse is free.

The great thing, wherever you stand as a poet, is to avoid the kind of dichotomies implied by such a statement. Metrics are not a device for restraining the mad, any more than 'open form' or free verse is a prairie where a man can do all kinds of manly things in a state of wholesome unrestrictedness.

I mentioned earlier a group of aspiring writers whose allegiance to an unexamined ideology of open form had left them short of a particular thing they wanted or needed: they had nothing to read to an audience, because they had written nothing with performance in mind. Because to write for performance was an offence against some unwritten code – although as it happened they also wanted to perform.

In this context I was interested to find, in a book about the history of the revolt against metre, that one of the things that had disgusted Ford Madox Ford, in contemplating the poets of his own day (that is, the late nineteenth century), was the way they behaved in performance. When they started to recite, said Ford, the most horrible changes overcame these normally nice people. They had all, always, on these occasions the aspects and voices, not only to [*sic*] awful High Priests before Drawing Room altars – but they held their heads at unnatural angles and appeared to be suffering the tortures of agonising souls. It was their voices that did that. They were doing what Tennyson calls, with admiration: 'Mouthing out their hollow O's and A's.'

And it went on and on – and on! A long, rolling stream, of words no one would ever use, to endless monotonous, polysyllabic, unchanging rhythms, in which rhymes went unmeaningly by like the telegraph posts, every fifty yards, of a railway journey.★

And it was these awful poets in performance who made him feel that there was something wrong with the mere framing of verse, the sound of it to the ear, that put people in a false frame of mind. And so Ford proposed for himself (and others) a verse written 'in exactly the same vocabulary as that which one used for one's prose';

that, if it were to be rhymed, the rhyme must never lead to the introduction of unnecessary thought; and, lastly, that no exigency of metre must interfere with the personal cadence of the writer's mind or the pressure of the recorded emotion.†

Hence, in his account, the move towards imagism and *vers libre*.

We recognize the feeling very well, but we are very unlikely, to say the least of it, to have sat through precisely that kind of poetry reading. Instead, the horribly transformed,

★ Quoted in *Missing Measures: Modern Poetry and the Revolt against Meter* by Timothy Steele (University of Arkansas Press, 1990), p. 38.
† Ibid., p. 39.

normally nice people who bore us to death are far more likely to be pouring out their thoughts in free verse. A century has passed, and many of the figures Ford felt impelled to revolt against, like Lewis Morris, are largely unknown to us, while others, like Tennyson, have lost their power to oppress us – and lost it long since. We come to a poem such as *In Memoriam* with a sense of wonder, perhaps even shock.

At the time Ford was talking about, there already existed a tradition of free verse, although it was not considered such. It was a tradition of vatic utterance, such as that represented by Blake – the Blake of the prophetic books. It was a tradition that drew sustenance from the sense that there were books in the Bible which, although not written metrically, constituted a kind of poetry. The Psalms, for instance, were clearly a kind of poetry, as was the Song of Solomon.

And when Whitman produced his *Leaves of Grass* (1855), one might see that, revolutionary in spirit though the poems were, they belonged to an old prophetic tradition. One might have been shocked at what Whitman said, but not I think at his mode of saying it, which, though unusual, would be recognizable as a sort of ecstatic religious outpouring.

By contrast the works of the imagists, which *said* for the most part nothing at all, but only presented experiences, were shocking or puzzling or risible to their early readers because, instead of that familiar vatic prolixity, they were extremely short and supposed to be denuded of artifice. To us today this kind of free verse seems moon-obsessed and affected. Here is the fifth of a series of 'Nocturnes' by Skipwith Cannell:

I am weary with love, and thy lips
Are night-born poppies.
Give me therefore thy lips
That I may know sleep.*

You may feel outraged at being expected to spend a decent
length of time in contemplation of something that can be
taken in, with all its defects, at a glance. But the imagists,
though often weak as poets, were influential, both as harbin-
gers of free verse and as minimalists. T. E. Hulme's 'Images'
may not all succeed:

Old houses were scaffolding once
          and workmen whistling.

      ★

Her skirt lifted as a dark mist
From the columns of amethyst.

      ★

Sounds fluttered,
       like bats in the dusk.

      ★

The flounced edge of skirt,
       recoiling like waves off a cliff.†

The first of these has found its way, on its own, into the *New
Penguin Book of English Verse*, and it can only have done so
because minimalist taste has so well established itself. Otherwise it is vulnerable to the objection that it is a good line for
a poem, not a good poem in itself. (Note by the way that the

* *Imagist Poetry*, ed. Peter Jones (Penguin, 1972), p. 59.
† Ibid., p. 49.

second of the poems contains an example of an off-beat rhyme of a kind mentioned in the chapter above on rhyme.)

So early free verse came in two contrasting guises: the extensive, prolix and ecstatic – well represented in the twentieth century by Allen Ginsberg; and the minimalist, stripped-down, freed of all artifice, short-lined and lower-cased, as in some famous works of William Carlos Williams. It was the free verse of this latter category that seemed to make war with traditional poetry. The poets who championed this revolution lived in the expectation (which was not fulfilled) that a new metrical understanding would supplant the old. They tried to see their free verse, as, in some way, metrical or scannable.

It would have been better, perhaps, to go on seeing it as free. Among the pioneers of free verse, D. H. Lawrence stands out as one who, though gifted in metrical verse, is happier without metre. He is happier when he is able to follow the rhythms of his conversation, his expostulations, his outraged thoughts. It is utterly unclear where his prose ends and his poetry begins – whether for instance his essay on Whitman is not really a poem to Whitman written out as prose – but this is the state of affairs with Lawrence, and there is not much point in regretting it.

Once the initial shock had been absorbed, the revolution effected by free verse began to look very democratic, as indeed it was in some of its aspects. Whitman was after all a democratic spirit. Modernism in other arts brought extreme difficulty. In poetry, the characteristic difficulty imported under the name of modernism was obscurity. But obscurity could just as easily be a quality of metrical as of free verse.

Free verse seemed democratic because it offered freedom of access to *writers*. And those who disdained free verse would always be open to accusations of elitism, mandarinism. Open form was like common ground on which all might graze their cattle – it was not to be closed in by usurping landlords.

One should say to the free spirits grazing their herds on open form: good luck, free spirits!

But if the land looks overgrazed, one should feel free to move on.

20. Writing for the Eye

Writing for the page is only one form of writing for the eye. Wherever solemn inscriptions are put up in public places, there is a sense that the site and the occasion demand a form of writing which goes beyond plain informative prose. Each word is so valued that the letters forming it are seen as objects of solemn beauty. They may not constitute poems, but the art of writing inscriptions might be seen as analogous to the writing of poetry.

The term epitaph itself means something to be spoken at a burial or engraved upon a tomb. When an epitaph is a poem written for a tomb, and appears in a book, we are aware that we are not reading it in its proper form: we are reading a reproduction. The original of the epitaph is the tomb itself, with its words cut into the stone.

The elaborate poems that decorate the tombs and memorials of old English churches have little currency outside their church setting (unless they happen to be comic or otherwise curious). They were written to be read when standing on a given spot in the church. And the criteria that went into the writing of them were special. Dr Johnson's remark that a man is not on oath when writing an epitaph bears this out. One does not expect a balanced judgement of a person's merits to be found in a church epitaph: one expects merits.

The modern epitaph is in abeyance though not dead. Philip Larkin's poems about the Humber Bridge and the university library in Hull are examples of poems to be read on the spot, celebrating the merits of the bridge and the library.

Any form of lettering that draws a particular attention to itself as lettering – the beautiful fonts of the Renaissance, the chunkiest sans serif scripts – may draw such attention to a sentence, a phrase, or a word, that it becomes an object of special aesthetic interest, and therefore something like a poem. The 'Image' by T. E. Hulme quoted in the last chapter may look vulnerable on the page:

> Old houses were scaffolding once
>   and workmen whistling.

Imagine it realized in neon light, on the wall of an art gallery, with a room to itself: we're in business.

On the following pages are some poems written for the page, Herbert's 'The Altar' and 'Easter Wings', in which the poems make pictures; an example from Lewis Carroll, in which the typography puns (but the poem is forced into the shape); and two from Edwin Morgan, his 'Orgy', which relies on sound as much as vision, and one of his extraordinary 'emergent poems', in which a line taken from Brecht generates a poem which can be read as a commentary on that line.

A broken ALTAR, Lord, thy servant rears,
Made of a heart, and cemented with tears:
  Whose parts are as thy hand did frame;
  No workman's tool hath touch'd the same.
      A   HEART   alone
      Is   such   a   stone,
      As   nothing   but
      Thy pow'r doth cut.
      Wherefore each part
      Of my hard heart
      Meets in this frame,
      To praise thy name.
  That if I chance to hold my peace,
  These stones to praise thee may not cease.
O let thy blessed SACRIFICE be mine,
And sanctify this ALTAR to be thine.

        (George Herbert, 'The Altar')

(1) (2)

My tender age in sorrow did begin:
And still with sicknesses and shame
Thou didst so punish sin,
That I became
Most thin.
With thee
Let me combine,
And feel this day thy victory:
For, if I imp my wing on thine,
Affliction shall advance the flight in me.

Lord, who createdst man in wealth and store,
Though foolishly he lost the same,
Decaying more and more,
Till he became
Most poor:
With thee
O let me rise
As larks, harmoniously,
And sing this day thy victories:
Then shall the fall further the flight in me.

(George Herbert, 'Easter Wings')

Fury said to
a mouse, That
he met in the
house, 'Let
us both go
to law: *I*
will prose-
cute *you.* –
Come, I'll
take no de-
nial: We
must have
the trial;
For really
this morn-
ing I've
nothing
to do.'
Said the
mouse to
the cur,
'Such a
trial, dear
sir, With
no jury
or judge,
would
be wast-
ing our
breath.'
'I'll be
judge,
I'll be
jury,'
said
cun-
ning
old
Fury:
'I'll
try
the
whole
cause,
and
con-
demn
you to
death.'

(Lewis Carroll,
Alice's Adventures in Wonderland)

```
      a                 l         l
           rea        ch
  d       e          a  t h
              a            l         l
    en   a              c t
  de           at         h
                    a                ll
      a              r                  e
          k                  i              n
      all       a       r                  e
    n     e       a       r              all
                          i     n
          re       a  c  h
                            on
              t  r        i      al
                          i     n
  den                     i        al
       a l                  on    e
                          il      l
                  b         on    e
    e    a     t                    en
      n    e   r                  v   e
           f          allen
                bra      i    n
    n           u        l       l
           a         h
      l                  i v      e
             bra           v      e
             b                    e
      a l               i  v      e
       le          a        v     e
      all           t        o
        l             i f       e
        l    ea              v      e
  dc    a      t        h
     n                        o
       a          r    t
  n                        o
              tur                    n
     n                        o
       a   rea
  n                          o
          u   r           n
            b  u  t
    e    a        ch
              b                    e
  d     e    a  r     t    o
        e    a        c  h
                    i         n
      a          l       l
```

denn alle kreatur braucht hilf von allen

(Edwin Morgan, 'Plea')

```
cantercantercantercanter
anteateranteateranteater
antencounterantencounter
antennareactantennareact
antantantantantantantant
antantantantantantantant
antantantantantantantant
antantantantantantantant
cantcountantcantcountant
anaccountantanaccountant
anteateranteateranteater
eateateateateateateateat
eateateateateateateateat
anteatenanteatenanteaten
nectarnectarnectarnectar
trancetrancetrancetrance
★★★★★★★★★★★★★★★★
canteatanantcanteatanant
anteatercantanteatercant
notanantnotanantnotanant
★★★★★★★★★★★★★★★★
trancetrancetrancetrance
ocontentocontentocontent
nocanternocanternocanter
```

(Edwin Morgan, 'Orgy')

21. Song

I have already said that in song the same rule applies as in dramatic verse: the meaning must yield itself, or yield itself sufficiently to arouse the attention and interest, in real time. As we hear the song, its meaning unfolds, and it must do so without asking us to refer back, as it were, to the top of the page. When we write a poem which we expect to be read rather than heard, maybe we begin to assume that the reader will take the opportunity to refer back, to look at the general disposition of lines on the page, to admire the way it looks as well as what it says. A poem thus designed could also contain intriguing verbal puzzles that only yield themselves to quiet scrutiny on the page. But a song may look like nothing at all, or it may look disappointing, and still be a great lyric.

Sometimes I have thought that a song *should* look disappointing on the page – a little thin, perhaps, a little repetitive, or a little on the obvious side, or a mixture of all of these things. What then happens, when it is handed to the composer, is that this area of disappointment, this sense of the poem's being insufficient on its own, becomes the very area in which the composer can work. What had looked *slightly* disappointing to the reader becomes *enormously* interesting to the composer. The composer does not want the self-sufficiency of a richly complex text: he or she wants to feel that the text is something in need of musical setting.

Of course, what the poet wants, and what the composer wants, do not have to be the same thing. If I think of Shakespeare's songs, I cannot identify this vulnerability, this insufficiency I have been talking about. 'When icicles hang

by the wall' is a first-rate poem vividly describing winter, one
of the best evocations of daily life from its period. It is not in
need of rescue by any composer. So I am forced to withdraw
the idea that a lyric *should* look disappointing and say instead
that it *can* look very disappointing indeed. Great music can be
set to the most banal words. The tune that used to be known
as 'Handel's Largo', beloved slow march of military bands,
and which is perhaps better known today as the aria *Ombra
mai fu*, has the most exiguous of lyrics:

> *Ombra mai fu*
> *Di vegetabile*
> *Caro ed amabile*
> *Soave più.*

Which the critic Eric Blom once saw translated as:

> Never was shade
> Of dear and amiable
> Vegetable
> More sweet.

A perfectly faithful translation, as he pointed out, but comic.
This brief text serves Handel for minutes of the most exquisite
music.

One sometimes feels that composers do not really need
words, but they do. If you listen to singers vocalizing, as they
are asked to do in some instrumental works, using no words
at all, the effect (though it can be lovely) is quite different
from that of a song or other sung text. And this is true, I
maintain, even when we do not understand the words we are
listening to. Genuine language, even when we do not know

what it means, sounds different from cod language, real words from nonsense words.

Composers need words, but they do not necessarily need poetry. The Russian composer, Aleksandr Mossolov, who chose texts from newspaper small ads, had a good point to make. With a revolutionary music, any text can be set to work.

From the poet's point of view, however, it is a matter of considerable interest what actually happens to his words, particularly if a work is being commissioned for a particular composer. A man wrote to me asking for a libretto, and enclosing a sample of his work. I replied thanking him for the sample and saying that if he chopped up and destroyed the words in that way then he didn't need a specially commissioned text. Any words would do.

Nevertheless, I said, a different poet might take a different view, and I mentioned the name of a friend who was an experienced librettist. The composer approached my friend, and recounted what I had said. But he had thought of a solution. He would set the words in his usual way, but the opera would be performed with surtitles as a matter of course. My friend thought this a reasonable solution to the problem, and the commission went happily ahead.

It went happily ahead because the situation was clear to both parties.

But here is another situation involving the same friend. He is asked to write a libretto for a so-called opera workshop, and does so. He and the composer and the director meet up for a discussion. The director says: Fine, the workshop can go ahead and you won't be needed for the next few weeks. My friend says: One moment – you may make all kinds of changes to my text, but such changes as are made must be made with my approval. A few days later he is told that the project is 'dead in the water'.

The two examples are enough to remind the poet, at the very least, to ask himself before any collaboration what terms he wants and can expect. Working alone on a poem, a poet is of all artists the most free. The poem can be written with a modicum of technology, and can be published, in most cases, quite cheaply.

What I want, when I write a poem, is no more than this: that it be preserved in some published form so that, in principle, someone somewhere will be able to find it and read it. That is all I need, as a poet, and that is the beauty, the luxury of my position. My lyric is mine and remains mine. Nobody can ruin it.

When I write a song, on the other hand, I must start to think of the implications of collaboration. Am I writing a poem which is to remain mine, as all my other poems do, or is it to be handed over, to become in some sense and to some degree someone else's property?

Some of the considerations involved are simply legal, and can be sorted out by an agent. But some of the considerations are artistic and need to be faced by the writer, if he is not to be driven mad with frustration and bitter with disappointment.

The optimum position is this: I write a song lyric which is, first and for ever, my own inalienable property. This means that I am free. Within my lyric I can do as I please, and it remains mine for ever. When a composer turns up who wants to use it, he may be given a licence to do so, but that licence is not exclusively his. In such circumstances, a composer cannot harm a song, because the text remains for ever mine. He may do a bad job. Another composer may come along and do a better one.

The disadvantage of this position may be untroubling to some poets: no composer may come along, no setting may ever be made. But to others this failure to be performed may feel like a catastrophe.

In that case, we need a composer, a collaboration. We need perhaps to sacrifice some of our sovereignty, our valued poetic independence.

People often want to know, when the subject of writing for music comes up, whether the music or the text comes first. If the music does indeed come first, then the lyricist had better think of this work as something rather less than poetry, for it is rather too much to expect that words fitted to pre-existent music can amount to much more than a very professional job.

Many musicals are written in this way, partly because many composers of musicals are not fully trained musicians. Their music arises from their improvisations at the keyboard, or whatever their instrument is. They cannot read or write music and they would be hard put to sit down with a text and examine its musical possibilities. Their gift is for devising a tune: others will set words to it, and others will provide an orchestration.

Where a lyricist is asked to provide words for existing music based on a translation of an existing libretto, the difficulty is compounded. If it had been the other way around, if the composer were devising music for given words, then it would be the composer's job to ensure that the end result is singable. That means ensuring that important notes carry important words, that the vowel-sounds are singable at a given pitch, and that if there are clusters of consonants they do not make the song into a tongue-twister. Of course if the lyricist is alive and well, he can be contacted and begged to alter a certain passage, but in principle it falls to the composer to make the whole thing feasible.

With a translation of lyrics or libretto, the assumption is that the music is already proved, tried and tested. The composer may well be dead. Even if he is not, a lyricist would be hard put to demand a change in something that has worked perfectly well in another language. So it is up to the lyricist to ensure singability.

But singability is not an exact science, as one quickly learns when listening to opera singers explaining what they can and cannot, will and will not, do given a certain passage. Each singer varies in his or her demands, but it may well be that the more amenable singer is only being amenable because she has no intention, in fact, on the night, of singing your words anyway. While the more difficult diva may well be being difficult because she really does intend that the text comes over loud and clear.

At all events, one is encouraged not to indulge illusions about artistic integrity. Singers can be quite ruthless at changing words, singing their own texts, substituting lines from old translations and so forth, and if they do not like your words your words will not survive.

Advice on lyrics given me years ago by the conductor Mark Elder seems worth pondering: if it shouts well, he said, it will probably sing well.

When the poet, the lyricist, is in the stronger position of writing the words before the music, that the words shout well should be easy to arrange. And it is possible, with certain kinds of musical commission, for the writer to work with some sort of provisional tune in his head, as a private guarantee that the words are singable in theory. Such a tune may be of the lyricist's own devising, or may be an existent melody. In either case it is better to give the composer no inkling of what you had in mind as you wrote the words – no hint of the idiom, tempo, anything at all about what was running through your head.

Because however much you as lyricist know that this music

was just a provisional music, which will as surely be dismantled by the composer as the scaffolding will be removed from a newly finished house, the composer may feel that you were acting ultra vires. You had trespassed beyond your remit in even *thinking* about the fact that there would be music at all.

Richard Strauss writes to his librettist Hugo von Hofmannsthal, at the beginning of their long, successful collaboration: 'There is only one thing I would ask you: when composing your text don't think of the music at all – I'll see to that.' And Hofmannsthal replies: 'Rest assured, my dear Dr Strauss, that over the whole text I shall rely upon myself alone and not at all on the music; this is indeed the only way in which we can and must collaborate.'★

But if Hofmannsthal had never thought about the music, there would have been no operas to speak of.

★ *A Working Friendship: The Correspondence between Richard Strauss and Hugo von Hofmannsthal*, translated by Hanns Hammelmann and Ewald Osers (Random House, 1961), pp. 12–13.

22. Poetic Drama and Opera

Considering the wealth of poetic drama that has come down to us from the Elizabethan and Jacobean periods, it is surprising that so little of any value has been added since. It is not that poets have not tried. On the contrary, in the eighteenth and nineteenth centuries innumerable verse dramas were written and indeed performed, but none of this survives in the English repertoire. Nor is this very likely to be a case of unjust neglect. Classical companies have often searched for abandoned theatrical masterpieces from this fallow period, but have failed to come up with much of interest after Otway's *Venice Preserved* (1682).

Nevertheless, poetic drama sometimes survives in modified forms. For instance, if Racine or Sophocles is to be performed on the English stage, a poetic translation will be needed, and since the idiom in which either of these playwrights wrote involved much that is very far from our own traditions, conscious poetic choices have to be made by the translator in order to find an idiom for the modern stage. Many poets have turned their hands to such work, which can be both an interesting challenge and a source of income (one of the rare sources of income for a poet which actually involves the writing of verse).

Another way in which poetic drama survives is by being set to music. We may never read Victor Hugo's play *Le Roi s'amuse*, but if we know Verdi's *Rigoletto* we know Hugo's play – abridged, transposed, transformed, but still very much, in the feel of it, his play. We may never get to see Hugo's

Hernani on the English stage, but Verdi's *Ernani* does indeed turn up in the repertoire.

In the same way, we may think we know nothing of Pushkin until we add up the number of musical adaptations of his work: *Eugene Onegin, Boris Godunov, Ruslan and Lyudmila, The Queen of Spades* . . . What is more, Tchaikovsky's *Onegin* not only makes us acquainted with the story and something of the atmosphere of Pushkin's work: it is a remarkable fact that, if you are familiar with the phrases of the music, you will also be familiar with Pushkin's measure – not the whole stanza, perhaps, but that characteristic four-foot line with its pattern of feminine and masculine endings. The composer incorporates such chunks of the original poem in his work, and sets them so audibly, that, without knowing a word of Russian, you will have a sense of the way the verse is constructed.

Schiller is a poet whose drama finds its way to us, this time disguised as Italian opera: *Luisa Miller, Maria Stuarda, Guglielmo Tell, I Masnadieri, Don Carlo, Giovanna d'Arco* . . . And if we think we know very little Goethe, we may be surprised to find how much has come to us through the medium of music, just as Shakespeare's and Byron's work has been transmitted musically through the non-English-speaking world.

All this should give us pause before we write off poetic drama as an extinct art form. One may say, Yes, I know the kind of thing that happens in opera, only too well, alas: the whole art is ridiculous, But it is *not* ridiculous to sing in drama, unless it is ridiculous, altogether, to raise our voices in song. And it is not ridiculous to think of writing poetic drama, unless it is also ridiculous to raise our voices in poetry.

What then is the source of our unease in the face of the term 'poetic drama'? Do we expect something pseudo-Shakespearean? That danger surely passed a long time ago. Or do we expect something which, while not necessarily written in verse, is poetic in the sense that it is anti-realistic, that it is symbolist, that it uses a specially ornate language, like Oscar Wilde's *Salome* (one of those plays which is only tolerable today as an opera)? Whatever horror lies at the back of our mind, the best thing is to search it out and examine it, because when we examine these horrors we find they lose their power to harm us.

For instance, I have a horror of choruses and 'verse-speaking', but when I examine this horror it is really a horror of Eliot's choruses in *Murder in the Cathedral* (1935) and the 'verse-speaking' pioneered by Anglicans in the middle of the last century, the Anglicans who got together to perform Eliot's plays and other poetic dramas of the period. I don't in the least have a horror of Auden's choruses from the same period (they are the best things in his plays), nor of Eliot's unfinished *Sweeney Agonistes*, which actually plays very well, even when performed by amateurs, and which was rightly said to anticipate much of the spirit of Pinter's (prose) drama.

We all have these horrors, which can be so hard to explain. I cannot bear verse dialogues of the eclogue form, whoever writes them, and yet there are other forms of pastoral I delight in. I would rather stay at home with a bad book than attend a brilliant performance of *The Cocktail Party*, but I would be delighted to find that someone had succeeded in writing a good poetic drama, or a great verse libretto for an opera.

For just as there was a time in English drama when it seemed natural that the bulk of a play should be written in verse, so also there was a time in the history of European opera when it seemed clear that the job of the composer was to serve the words of the poet well. After all, the original impetus behind opera had been the urge to rediscover the lost mode of drama of the Greeks. So at the heart of the musical concept was the poetic text. But in due course, over the years, the poets in the world of opera lost caste, and we became hacks and drudges and garret-dwellers. And at the same time the composers became more and more overweening, so that Bellini felt entitled to set the police onto his librettist Romani, in order to ensure that a deadline was met.

What this means is that there is ground lying idle. As poets, we have a title to assert – a part of our inheritance lies unclaimed. And the way we assert our title is by writing. The way we refute, say, the death of the sonnet, or the reported demise of the epic, is not by argument but by assertion. My sonnet asserts that the sonnet still lives. My epic, should such fortune befall me, asserts that the heroic narrative is not lost – that it is born again, perhaps in some form which seems hardly at first recognizable, but nevertheless, there it is, born again.

As poets we do not ask permission before we begin to practise, for there is no authority to license us. We do not inquire whether it is still possible to pen a drama, for the answer to that question is ours alone to give. It is our drama, spoken or sung, that asserts our right to the title of poet. It is our decision that counts, and not the opinion of some theatre management, or the ponderings of the critic, or even the advice of our friendliest mentors. It is our decision, our assertion, that alters the whole state of affairs.

This is possible, we assert, because this is what I have just done. This is achievable, because I wanted enough to achieve it.

Glossary

accent: 'A superior force of voice, or of articulative effort, upon some particular syllable.' The old Webster's definition, quoted by the critic George Saintsbury, has great merit. The problem in the discussion of poetry is to distinguish between accent and stress, when in conversation the two words are often used as equivalents. The distinction I find useful to make is as follows.

With any word of more than one syllable – 'conversation', for instance – one of the syllables is liable to be accentuated. The accent in 'conversation' is on the third syllable, and is on that syllable every time we use the word. Whether we lay any *stress* on the word 'conversation' depends on the sentence in which it falls. 'His *accent* was atrocious, but his *conversation* was always memorable': the italics in such a sentence tell us to stress the two words so singled out. However, the way we actually stress such words is not to emphasize every syllable written in italics. It is to lay extra emphasis on the normally accented syllable.

The stress we give to a word is to do with its meaning: we give the word extra semantic weight. But the accented syllable of a word has, by itself, no such extra weight of meaning.

The patterns of English metre are accentual. A metrical poem is made up of words pronounced in their normal way, whose accented syllables coincide more or less accurately with the metrical pattern. If a word has to be mispronounced in order to fit the pattern, the poem is either bad or deliberately comic, or in some other way disruptive of normal practice.

The iambic pentameter very often contains four natural conversational stresses. There is an interplay between patterns of stress and metrical accent. It is also possible to write a poetic line counting only the stresses. Traditional ballad metre is a stress metre.

acrostic: A poem the first letters of whose lines spell, for example, the name of the subject of the poem. I wrote the following example as a poster poem, to celebrate the opening of Tate Modern:

This turbine hall, these galleries of light
Are freighted with a purpose and a power.
This bridge is like a contract and this tower
Evidence of a legacy, a right.

Massive with possibility they stand
Open to such surprise as may exist
Deep in the pulse, the chambers of the heart,
Exacting fresh precision from the hand,
Risk in the brush, resilience in the wrist.
New thoughts to paint, new passions to impart.

A Petrarchan sonnet, minus the first four lines.

alexandrine: A line of six iambic feet, used in English poetry in order (a) to create variety; (b) to provide a long line in a stanza of differing line-lengths.

alliteration: In metrical terms, an alliterative metre requires a certain number of words in each line to begin with the same letter. This Anglo-Saxon system of versification was carried over into Middle English and can be seen in the example from *Sir Gawain* in the first chapter. Attempts to revive such a system of versification have not usually been happy.

amphibrach: Ti-tum-ti, a foot made familiar by the limerick, whose first line consists of three amphibrachs.

anapaest: Ti-ti-tum, a foot with two short syllables before one long:

> When you're wounded and left on Afghanistan's plains,
> And the women come out to cut up what remains,
> Jest roll to your rifle and blow out your brains
>   An' go to your Gawd like a soldier.

> (Rudyard Kipling, 'The Young British Soldier')

assonance: 'An imperfect form of rhyme which counts only the vowel sound of the chief rhyming syllable.' Saintsbury's definition may be good and accurate, but you may find the word used to refer to any rough sort of half-rhyme.

ballad: A word of several meanings. In the history of English poetry it refers to the narrative poems, orally transmitted and, traditionally, sung.

ballad metre: A quatrain in which line 2 rhymes with line 4. Lines 1 and 3 have four stresses, lines 2 and 4 have three.

blank verse: Unrhymed iambic pentameters, the staple of the long English poem and much verse drama.

burden: In common usage, 'the burden of his song' means his message. In the context of prosody, the burden means the refrain. Of course the refrain often contains the message:

> And this the burden of his song
> For ever used to be:
> I care for nobody,
> No, not I,
> And nobody cares for me.

> (Isaac Bickerstaffe, 'The Jolly Miller',
> from *Love in a Village*)

Burns metre: A distinctive stanza form associated with Robert Burns, rhyming a-a-a-b-a-b, the a-lines consisting of iambic tetrameters and the b-lines of iambic dimeters.

caesura: A break within the poetic line. In English poetry, this can occur anywhere in the line.

catalectic: Lacking the last syllable. 'Lay your sleeping head, my love' is a trochaic tetrameter catalectic.

choriamb: A metre formed by placing a trochee in front of an iamb: Tum-ti-ti-tum. Rare in English practice as a genuine metre. Just because the line 'Whether 'tis nobler in the mind to suffer' begins with a trochee followed by an iamb, that does not mean that it is useful to say it begins with a choriamb. The useful thing is to look at the whole metrical context and ask: what is the metre here? Is it the iambic pentameter, or is there a regular repeating choriambic effect? If the latter, you might be reading Swinburne.

couplet: A group of two poetic lines, often rhyming.

dactyl: Tum-ti-ti, a metre associated with Latin poetry.

dimeter: A line consisting of two poetic feet.

doggerel: A type of bad poetry in which the demands of rhythm and rhyme have taken precedence over the choice of words. A poem, however, may enjoy assertive rhythms and upfront rhymes without being doggerel, which is always a kind of inept versification.

elision: The running together of two words by the omission of a syllable. In classical poetry there are rules for elision. In English poetry this is not the case. Different practices have been adopted in different periods.

end-stopped: An end-stopped line ends with a pause, however brief, often indicated by a punctuation mark.

enjambment: The running of one line on to the next without a pause.

feminine rhyme: The accented syllable is the penultimate or antepenultimate: handy rhyming with candy.

foot: In order to understand the construction of a line of verse, we divide it into feet, which are its constituent metrical units. One iamb equals one foot, and so forth.

fourteener: A line of seven iambic feet. Very easily it will split into four feet followed by three, in which case it is called ballad metre.

heroic couplets: A poem written in pairs of rhymed iambic pentameters is said to be in heroic couplets.

hexameter: A line of six feet.

iamb: Ti-tum, a foot of two syllables, the most important unit of English poetry.

light verse: Even Milton wrote some. Don't hold it against us.

line: In oral poetry, a line would have to be considered as a metrical unit, normally a given number of stresses or feet. Traditionally, in English poetry, the ending of the line is marked by a rhyme-word. In some ancient manuscripts it may be that a text was written without line-breaks or indications of stanza form: these have to be inferred from the metre. In modern written poetry, a line may vary in length from one syllable to a large number of words, with no apparent metre and with only the typography giving a clue as to the whereabouts of the line-ending.

masculine rhyme: The final syllable of the line is accented, so the rhyme is single and therefore deemed strong.

measure: A pleasant old word for metre.

metre: Think of metre as the *repeating* pattern (whether you think in terms of accent, stress or quantity) in a poem, and you will avoid getting bogged down in semantic disputes. English metrics are tolerant of wide degrees of variation, and sometimes when you focus on an individual line it may be unclear how it is supposed to scan. The best clue is in other similar lines. For instance, most characters in Shakespeare speak either in prose or in iambics, most of the time. Do not expect them to swerve off into choriambocretics.

monometer: A line consisting of a single foot.

octave: A verse of eight lines.

odes: The legendary occupation of the poet is the composing of an Ode, conceived as a grand effusion upon a grand occasion or a lofty theme. Oddly, there is no fixed idea of what form such an ode should take. The scansion of the Greek and Latin originals proved hard to imitate in English, so the best in that direction could only be an approximation to, say, Horace or Pindar. Marvell's 'Horatian ode' on Cromwell's return from Ireland is printed as a continuous series of alternating iambic couplets, first tetrameters, then trimeters. Collins's beautiful unrhymed 'Ode to Evening' has two lines of iambic pentameter followed by two trimeters; it seems the poet was unsure whether it should be printed as a continuous block or in stanzas (the sentences overrun the stanza form). Coleridge's incomparable 'Dejection' is an 'irregular ode', which means that the author can do as he wishes. Keats's odes are in beautiful regular stanzas. In other words, the field is open.

ottava rima: A stanza of eight iambic pentameters rhyming a–b–a–b–a–b–c–c.

pentameter: A line of five feet.

quantity: In ancient Greek poetry, syllables are distinguished by being long or short, according to whether they contain long or short vowels, and whether they end in a consonant. Latin poetry, in a way that is hard to comprehend, imitated this Greek system. English poetry simply cannot do so. But during the centuries in which a classical education was dominant in Europe, the educated classes learned to write poetry in Latin and Greek, and there was a great desire to carry over classical forms into English. Effectively this means translating a quantitative system into an accentual metre.

   To accuse an English poet of 'false quantities' is, strictly speaking, a *faux pas*.

quatrain: A stanza of four lines.

refrain: A line or verse repeated after each section of a song.

rhyme: Rhyme typically marks the end of the line with word-endings that contain identical vowel sounds and following consonant(s), but different consonants before the vowel. Cat rhymes with mat, but cat does not (in normal English) rhyme with khat, because the initial consonant would come out the same. Plain does not rhyme with plane, because it is aurally identical. Annoyingly enough, plane does not rhyme with explain: the relevant syllables are identical.

rhyme-royal: An abridged form of ottava rima, rhyming a-b-a-b-b-c-c.

rhythm: Note the difference between the vague use of this word in connection with the sense of movement, of stress or accent or beat, in poetry, and the precise use of the term in music. Musical rhythm takes place in time. One can count the beat. *Some* poems are written in this way (MacNeice's 'Bagpipe Music', Edith Sitwell's *Façade*, Auden's 'Night Mail') but most are not. Hamlet can take a long drag on a cigarette between 'To be or not to be' and 'that is the question' without offending against the scansion of the speech. If Calaf pulled the same stunt in '*Nessun dorma*' he would be sacked.

Sapphics: The most tempting of the classical metres. Catullus, imitating a poem of Sappho, gives an example:

> *Ille mi par esse deo videtur,*
> *ille, si fas est, superare divos,*
> *qui sedens adversus identidem te*
> *spectat et audit*

Any English quatrain in which the last line is indented in this way and sounds like 'Tum-ti-ti tum-tum' is probably an attempt at Sapphics. But how are the previous three lines scanned? Here is how the Latin metre is set out for readers of Catullus:

This reveals the difficulty of imitating classical models: three accented syllables in a row in a normal line would be impossible for us. In Latin these are three long syllables, a different matter (*see* **quantity**).

sestet: The latter part of a sonnet.

sestina: See Chapter 16.

sonnet: A poem of fourteen lines, normally iambic pentameters. For the different rhyme-schemes of the different kinds of sonnet, see Chapter 15.

stanza: A verse of a poem, that is to say a group of lines of a given rhyme-scheme and set of line-lengths which is then repeated. If the sections of the poem do not repeat themselves, in formal terms, more or less exactly, then the poem is not in stanzas but in an irregular form.

stress: *See* **accent**.

tercet: The group of three rhyming lines which is the basic unit of terza rima.

terza rima: Dante's narrative form in *The Divine Comedy*.

tetrameter: A line of four feet.

triolet: See Chapter 16.

triplet: A group of three poetic lines, often rhyming, as for instance the **tercet**.

trochee: Tum-ti, a two-syllable foot, the reverse of the iamb.

verse: (a) As opposed to prose, a composition employing metre and (usually) rhyme; (b) a subdivision of for instance a psalm or a song. Psalms, which are Hebrew religious songs, in the form made familiar in English translation through the Bible and the Prayer Book, were not metrical. However, many metrical versions were also made. A verse, in sense (b), may therefore be metrical or not.

verse paragraph: By analogy with prose, a group of lines in a long, normally unrhymed poem, to be taken together as having some kind of unity of theme.

villanelle: See examples by W. E. Henley and Dylan Thomas in Chapter 3.

Index

Acknowledgements

The Publishers wish to thank the following copyright-holders for permission to quote copyrighted material:

'Twelve Songs II and VI (Autumn Song)' from W. H. Auden: *Collected Poems*. Reprinted by permission of Faber & Faber.

Lines from 'Letter to Lord Byron' by W. H. Auden, from *The English Auden*. Reprinted by permission of Faber & Faber.

Lines from 'Waking Early Sunday Morning' from Robert Lowell: *Collected Poems*. Reprinted by permission of Faber & Faber.

Lines from 'The Whitsun Weddings' from Philip Larkin: *Collected Poems*. Reprinted by permission of Faber & Faber.

'Fly' by Christopher Reid, from *Expanded Universes*. Reprinted by permission of Faber & Faber.

Lines from 'Virginia Britannia' from Marianne Moore: *Collected Poems*. Reprinted by permission of Faber & Faber.

'Valentine' by Wendy Cope from *Serious Concerns*. Reprinted by permission of Faber & Faber.

Extract from Helen Vendler's introduction to *The Faber Book of Contemporary American Poetry*. Reprinted by permission of Faber & Faber.

Lines from 'Saltbush Bill' by A. B. 'Banjo' Paterson from *Banjo Paterson Favourites*. Copyright © Penguin Books, Australia, 1992.

'Plea' and 'Orgy' from Edwin Morgan: *Collected Poems*. Reprinted by permission of Carcanet Press Limited.

Lines from 'We've Got Cholera in Camp', 'Sestina of the Tramp-Royal' and 'The Young British Soldier' reprinted by permission of A. P. Watt Ltd on behalf of The National Trust for Places of Historical Interest or Natural Beauty.

'See the Spring', 'The Illusionists' and 'The Kiss' from John Fuller: *Collected Poems*, published by Chatto & Windus. Reprinted by permission of The Random House Group Ltd.

'Do Not Go Gentle Into That Good Night' from Dylan Thomas: *Collected Poems*, published by J. M. Dent. Reprinted by permission of David Higham Associates.

'When Gauguin was visiting Fiji' by Robert Conquest. Reprinted by permission of The Curtis Brown Group Ltd.

Every effort has been made to trace or contact all copyright-holders. The publishers will be pleased to make good any omissions or rectify any mistakes brought to their attention at the earliest opportunity.